SAM'S SCRAPBOOK
MY MOTORSPORTS MEMORIES

Published in August 2021

ISBN 978-1-910505-65-6

Published by Evro Publishing
Westrow House, Holwell, Sherborne, Dorset DT9 5LF, UK

www.evropublishing.com

Edited by Mark Hughes
Designed by Richard Parsons

Printed and bound in Slovenia by GPS Group

Front cover photograph by Ellen Griesedieck

SAM'S SCRAPBOOK

MY MOTORSPORTS MEMORIES

SAM POSEY WITH JOHN POSEY

EVRO
PUBLISHING

Contents

Fill'er up!

Here's my son John helping me out, as he has
done, selflessly, for his whole life. His work on
this book is a recent example. From the day he
started transcribing my stories, he showed his
rare ability to write and edit at the same time.

I couldn't have done it without him.

Introduction

I met Sam somewhere around 1975, when I was just 10 years old. My dad brought me to a race and it was a real thrill meeting these drivers in person. At the time I didn't know much about the sport or the personalities, but I knew I was hooked. Sam was gracious and happy to meet his fans, and even signed my poster!

Fast forward a few decades and now I'm behind the wheel of my very own racecars but, of course, not nearly to the level of what Sam has achieved. When I think of myself as that aspiring 10-year-old racecar driver, I remember how gracious Sam was to me so many years before.

It turns out, Sam doesn't live too far from me. Over the years I have gotten to know him and his family much better. I cherish the events we attend together and my visits to his art studio. During one of our Saturday lunches, while listening to Sam's stories and looking at pictures, I mentioned this idea of a scrapbook. I hope it brings you closer to these stories and that you enjoy reading it as much as I've enjoyed being a part of it.

Bob D'Amato

Dreams of glory
Mudge Pond Express

Mudge Pond is about half a mile from where my grandparents lived, downhill through the woods. During the depression, my grandfather came up with the somewhat impractical project of a road from his house to the pond, consisting of two concrete tracks 18 inches wide with four feet between them, so you could put one set of a car's wheels on each side. He thought he could provide employment to some people in our town, and that his family would enjoy the road.

When my friend John Whitman and I were 12, we had a sled with wheels on it that you kneeled on, either coasting or propelling yourself by pushing off the ground with your other foot. You steered it with two metal handles that stuck out from under the body and moved the front wheels, and you could brake by pressing the handles on the wheels or by dragging your feet. The tires were hard rubber, half an inch wide. We called it the Mudge Pond Express because we dreamed of using it to coast along my grandfather's road all the way to the lake.

The Express just fit on one of the two lanes. The first section was straight, about 150 feet to the first turn. The turns were paved in between the lanes, so you could take a line. At a beach tree just past the turn, the track flattened out and we ran out of steam. At the end of the straight, I built a ramp about four feet long and four feet high, imagining how we would soar into the air, but we never built up enough momentum to climb the ramp.

Looking for a greater sense of speed, we next took the Express to my mother's basement. It was large and cool and well lit — perfect for intense exercise. The start/finish was at the freezer door about halfway along the north side of the house. The first turn was a right-hand swerve, very fast. You hit a short straight — about three feet — and then went right around a lolly column into the shop area, setting up for the bench turn, which posed the danger of a protruding clamp. From there you had to negotiate a hairpin, another column, the ping-pong table, and a double-apex left-hander under the electrical box, which brought you back to the freezer. You had to be careful cornering hard, as your outside shoulder was well beyond the wheels.

Whenever Johnny visited, we headed for the basement, where we could stay for a few hours. We timed the runs with a stopwatch. Johnny was far more athletic, and I'm sure he won almost all the events; it was more a question of how far back I finished. But I found I had a certain aptitude for this kind of thing, and I did better than we might have expected.

A second event, following the same course: we put down two lines of masking tape on the floor, about a foot apart, to create a track for our Schuco cars — very heavy models about two inches long of Grand Prix cars of the Fangio era — and pulled them behind us with strings attached to their noses. After enough laps, you developed a precise sequence of movements — right, left, hesitation, left — a complex choreography of dips and lunges, sprints and stops that could become hypnotic after 20 minutes straight — not so different than driving Monaco.

We raced one at a time against the watch. Just as Formula One drivers are now penalized for going out of the track into the runoff areas, a second was added to your time

HONOR MEMBER

Automobile Club of New York

28 EAST 78TH ST. AT MADISON AVE. NEW YORK 21, N. Y.

Mrs. Samuel W. Moore

is a Regular Member, and as provided by the By-Laws, is entitled
to all Club privileges. This card is valid until MAY 31, 1962

N⁰ 953175

President

when all four wheels went outside the tape. On your honor, you called your own penalties with a shout of "Fault!"

It all seemed very logical, and in fact it did place some fairly stringent demands on coordination and concentration, as well as stamina, as some of our endurance races lasted an hour.

From upstairs, my mother's only experience of these events was the sound of our pounding feet and "fault." She never came down to stop us. My mother was an excellent driver, a member of the Automobile Club of New York. She would show the same support for the rest of my career.

Outside the basement, we would pore over *Autocourse* and every issue of *Competition Press*. We even wrote up quizzes to test each other's knowledge. Note that the second sample is from section 14. The answers can be found on pages 158–159.

In these photos, we're reenacting the events for my first book.

4. Identify the following designations. There is only one car for each designation.

105 E	17-M
GTL	PL 17
PY-544	
211	2-CV
541-R	4-CV
12-M	
RS-21	K 3
3.2	T. 3
HBR-5	
S-440	122 S
PV-444-L	S-2
7	
170	46
C.N.7	246
30	
96	
360	(Total of Twenty-Seven)

5. Which of the following should properly be hyphenated?

Ace Bristol	Super America	
Alfa Romeo	Fiat Abarth	
Aston Martin	Hillman Minx	(Total of
Austin Healey	Mercedes Benz	Thirteen)
Deutsch Bonnet	Rolls Royce	
Auto Union	Lister Jaguar	
Facel Vega		

14. Random Questions.

a) What to the nearest 5 hp was the power output of the Ward Lime Rock midget?
b) What three men are responsible for the Echidna?
c) What is Ugolini's first name?
d) Basically, is the GP Cooper an understeering or oversteering car?
e) Who is Jacques Washer?
f) Who is generally considered the best driver in town-to-town long-distance races, and who wore that crown before him?
g) Before the 1959 Portuguese GP, only two GP drivers had ever driven the Monsanto circuit before. Who were they?
h) When & where did Gendebien first drive in a championship Grand Epreuve?
i) What is meant by the "Gran Premio Nuvolari"?
j) Who was known as Oberingenieur?
k) Who is responsible for Lola? Sting Ray?
l) What was the smallest (engine displacement) car ever to win Le Mans?
m) Name two double & two triple winners at Le Mans.
n) At what famous GP did Nuvolari attempt to steer a burning car with his dogs?
o) What was the "famous pitstop where everything went wrong?
p) What driver lost an ear and had a (over to next)

11

First car
Mercedes 300 SL

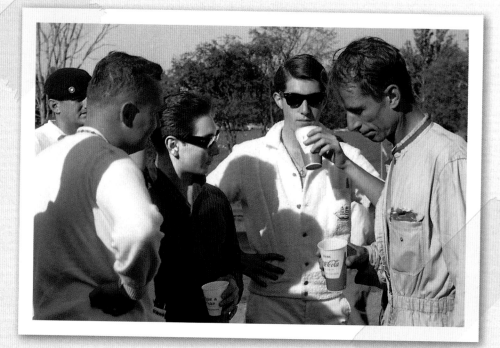

Here you see John Fitch talking with Pedro Rodriguez at a 1958 USAC race at Lime Rock. These men were legends to me. John was a veteran of Le Mans and the Mille Miglia, as well as a pilot who was shot down over Germany in World War II and survived. He also had a dealership not far from where we lived. I was 14 when I heard that he had a Mercedes 300 SL in his showroom. I asked my mom to go see it. It was so beautiful that I immediately said let's buy it, having no idea what it cost.

The salesman let us take it out. Once we were out of his sight, my mom pulled over and let me drive. I felt obliged to take the car up to its top speed. It had a very tight gear ratio, better for acceleration. I think it hit 145. They were asking $2,500 for it. They let us take it home while we thought it over.

I had money my father had left me. But my mom didn't think it would be a good image for me, at 14, to have a car of this kind. She was in the kitchen, debating, while I drove around and around the circle of our driveway. Finally, she came out and said, "I'm going to let you buy it, because I believe if your dad was alive now, he would want you to have it."

The SL was superior in performance to anything else of the time that wasn't a pure racing car. And it had raced against the best cars built for racing. Now of course an average family sedan can match its performance. But it remains my symbol of a supercar. It helped build the reputation of Mercedes, represented the return of Germany after the war. In 1955, Mercedes had dominated Formula One and the sports-car

championship, and John Fitch had just driven an SL to fifth in the Mille Miglia. I felt I was one step away from that world of romance.

I still didn't have a driver's license, but no one said I couldn't drive the car on our own property. My uncle had built an airstrip behind the house that he used with his Grumman Widgeon.

The SL has an unusual pedal arrangement that made the heel-toe maneuver more difficult. The car had a full belly pan, not much ground clearance, but I didn't care. I pounded around the airstrip, practicing my downshifts. At least I had nothing to hit. I would just steer from side to side, feeling the bite of the tires.

I still have the car today, shown here at Lime Rock in some recent photos.

Jocko
Lime Rock, 1964

Because my mom had bought a share of stock in the track at Lime Rock, I was able to drive there before I was 21. We never considered taking out the SL. Our friend Jim Haynes suggested that I look at something called the Jocko — named for its builder, Jocko Maggiacomo, who had earned a medal of honor from President Johnson when he rescued another driver from a flaming wreck in the middle of a race. The car was red and front-engined. If you closed your eyes and worked your imagination a little, it could almost be Fangio's Maserati. Maggiacomo's brave act seemed to give the car added cachet. I bought it for $1,000.

The first day I had it on the track, I did some drifting, a wonderful experience — the front wheels turning one way as the car went the other, the whole car flexing and feeling alive underneath you. The Jocko understeered going into West Bend, the turn just before the bridge, and oversteered savagely going out. Another disconcerting feature was that the drivetrain ran right between your legs. After a few laps, the carburetors started leaking fuel onto the exhaust pipes. I pulled off just after Big Bend and by chance found a two-by-six about four feet long lying in the grass. I put it on top of the carburetors, so the fuel leaked onto the wood instead of the exhaust, and drove carefully back to the pits. Here Jim Haynes sits in the car on the grid

at Lime Rock. After inspecting it more closely, he suggested I sell it. The new owner paid $1,000.

The car still exists today, restored to immaculate condition by its current owner, Neil Tolich, who did so well racing it around his home in New Zealand that he earned an entry into the prestigious vintage event at Monaco held every year the week before the grand prix.

First race
Lime Rock, 1964

In the fall of my senior year at college, John Fitch had some Formcars — Formula Vees with 44 horsepower — for sale and was eager to sell me one. He was going to be racing his at Lime Rock one Saturday and invited me to drive it in practice the Friday before.

I had to take an English exam that morning and then turn in my art portfolio. From there, I drove the three hours to the office of my family's lawyer in New York, where we worked out a plan for how to use my inheritance to finance the start of a racing career. I drove from there to the track, changed into a primitive suit, and got in the car with about ten minutes left before the end of practice. On the first full lap, I set the Formula Vee lap record. On the next, I went wide coming out of West Bend, spun off the inside, and nosed into the wall.

I was devastated. I had come straight from a meeting planning out the first steps for my future career — a plan that involved spending all the money I had. I had no girlfriend, no ambitions outside of racing; I had reached a point of almost desperate focus on my first race. And now I'd had my first crash, and in John Fitch's car. I couldn't put it in perspective, but John did. He told me I was fast, and he could fix the car that night. He won the race the next day.

In the rest of my career at Lime Rock, I crashed almost everywhere, but never again in West Bend.

That summer, I bought a Formcar from John and took it out at Lime Rock on free practice on Tuesdays. At the time,

you had to be 21 to race in the SCCA. I lied on a form (with my mother's backing) and did my first race at 20. I blew the start and in a frenzy tried to recoup the lost places by cutting across the esses. The runoff areas were rough. The car popped out of gear. I returned to the track well behind.

I finished fourth, but afterward the relief was immense. Until that moment, I'd been so desperate to be a racing driver, and I'd done everything in my power to make it a reality, but I hadn't driven a race. In those days, a group of enthusiasts would often come back from the track with us, talking over the events of the day. I stayed up with them well into the night.

I got a few more races in that summer but was still going off the track too often. John Fitch took me aside. "The racing, Sam," he said, "is on the black stuff." I won my first race at the end of the summer at Lime Rock in this Kelly, a faster version of the Formcar.

Reserve driver
Alfa Romeo GTZ, Bridgehampton, 1965

Harry Theodoracopulos was a Greek shipowner who loved to race. Erwin Hensey prepared Harry's cars. I got to know Erwin, a champion motorcycle racer in Germany before the war, because he worked at our local town garage.

Harry had an Alfa Romeo GTZ for the Double 500 at Bridgehampton, an important international race. I had driven just enough races to qualify for an international license. Through Erwin, I became the reserve driver.

Harry drove first, got about a quarter of the way into the race, and pitted. The exhaust fumes were making him woozy. Bob Grossman was our second driver. Bob was a Ferrari dealer, a great guy, and never made a mistake. He drove next and didn't get any farther than Harry. Everyone looked at me.

The cockpit was full of smoke. These two guys hadn't done more than ten laps each. I felt destiny knocking at my door. I drove out of the pits knowing I was going to finish the race.

The car had a little wing window that I could hold open on the straights with one hand, letting in just enough air to clear the cockpit. Near the end of the race, we were second in class behind the Porsche dealer Bert Everett. In this shot, I had just run out of gas. I pushed the car about a quarter of a mile back around to the pits and got one more lap in. Meanwhile, Everett had built a massive lead. But on the last lap, he broke down, giving us the win.

That night, Harry took me around to a series of parties at the mansions of his friends in East Hampton. I was in the fourth month of my career, and I'd won an international race.

Fédération Internationale de l'Automobile

AUTOMOBILE COMPETITION COMMITTEE FOR THE UNITED STATES, FIA, INC.

LICENSE FOR A DRIVER

No. 15025

Valid Until
12/31/65

Revalidated Until   *Revalidated Until*
DEC 31 1965

Revalidated Until   *Revalidated Until*

Daytona 24 Hours, 1966
Porsche 904 GTS

A few months later, Daytona was holding its first 24-hour race. I hadn't driven since Bridgehampton. Harry knew someone at Porsche who would sell us a 904 for $5,000. I was lucky enough to be able to write the check.

Our co-driver was Jim Haynes. Jim knew a Goodyear distributor, a wonderful man who died young only a few years later. We had Goodyear tires, and the works team had Dunlops. The Goodyears were far superior.

I drove first, hanging in with the factory cars. After three hours, Jim took over and did the same. Then it was Harry's turn. But by now it was dark, and Harry said he would rather wait for the morning. Jim and I traded the car through the night.

Erwin Hensey was a great mechanic, but he had no knowledge about that particular car. He never changed the brake pads. Around dawn, Jim came into the pits with no brakes — they had worn through the backing plates. It took us three quarters of an hour to change them. In this time, Harry had returned from his hotel, ready to take over.

All three of us had driven the car in practice. The first time you see it, the Daytona banking can look like a wall staring you in the face. Once you get through it, you know that you can, but Harry hadn't gotten through it. He'd approached me after his practice session: "On the banking, Sam, do you *leeft*?" Now I asked whether he felt more confident. He said no, he didn't, but he was ready to try.

In our class, cars were passing us and we were passing

them. You had to have a sixth sense for where they were, and you had to be decisive. I'd paid for the car, but Harry had secured the deal. He'd given me my ride at Bridgehampton. I looked up to him. But after the brake failure, I was more aware that the car could fail. I knew that if Harry got in, the race was over. I felt Jim and I had come too far to let it go.

I didn't know that by the time we fixed the brakes, we would be out of contention anyway. Jim and I finished the race. But first, Harry and I had an incredible argument. I grew up in the course of it, as he said some things to me that no one had before, and to my own surprise, I didn't back down.

In the end, the real hero of our race was my friend John Whitman. He timed every car, for every lap, for 24 hours, with one Hauer stopwatch. As far as I know, he was the first to achieve that feat.

Later that summer, Harry and I had patched up our rift. We won a big race, the Marlboro 12 hours outside of Washington. But the timers had missed a lap and had us second. John Whitman had again timed the entire race. He was also a lawyer. He stayed up from the finish at midnight until 3 a.m. and won our case.

In those days, my younger brothers and I still had a slot-car track at my mom's house. We painted up a few cars to look the ones I was driving.

John Whitman

Bizzarrini
Le Mans 24 Hours, 1966

Bizzarrini was an Italian car manufacturer founded by a former engineer for Ferrari and Alfa Romeo, Giotto Bizzarrini. John Fitch wanted to sell the cars in the US and thought it would help to have an American drive one at Le Mans. For someone of my record, the ride was way over my head, but he offered it to me anyway.

I was a babe in the woods. I went over with my mother and my brother Nick. We had no idea where to stay. As far as we could tell, the hotels were all full. We ended up in the basement of a private house. It rained like hell and the basement was pretty damp. We didn't have directions to the track, but we drove around in our rental car until I recognized that we were on the Mulsanne straight; we'd entered around Tertre Rouge. We drove down the three miles of it, along with trucks and farm machinery. I was thrilled out of my mind.

I didn't know where the team was staying, where the car was. They didn't know anything about me. We found them in some garage, I'm not sure how. There we met Bizzarrini himself. He turned out to be a very special guy, a professor at the University of Pisa. Although I didn't grasp it at the time, the entire crew was two students he'd picked from the university, for a team of two cars — my coupe and an open sports car. The open car was considered the faster of the two.

Whatever time they had was going into the sports car. I was so clueless that I didn't realize they hadn't installed seatbelts. My car was stock, handbuilt, one of about ten.

They didn't want to put many laps on the car, so I only had a few laps in practice. The rest of the time, I was at loose ends. But I qualified faster than the open car. After that, I sensed that the team had confidence in me.

My suit was cloth soaked in Borax, which was thought to resist fire. My helmet was as thick as cardboard. I was about to become the youngest American at the time to drive Le Mans, a source of pride ever since.

In those days, at the start, the drivers stood in circles about two feet across on a diagonal to their cars. When the gun went off, you ran to your car. With the coupe, I couldn't just vault in, and I was a little slow to get away. A man named Edgar Berney was driving the open car. Even with a cast on his right foot, he got going before I did. But his foot stuck on the gas, causing a burst of acceleration. As he swerved to avoid someone in front of me, I swerved to squeeze between him and the wall. We passed a few inches apart, the two Bizzarrinis almost taking each other out in the first hundred yards.

The next incident came at the end of the Mulsanne on the first lap. When I tried to brake, the pedal went to the floor. The crew hadn't told me that the brakes were new and the two students hadn't had a chance to bed them in. In the split second I had to think, I couldn't bear to take the escape road, which would mean some kind of time penalty. I geared down and tried to make the turn. I went up on the bank outside of it, staying on the gas so I wouldn't get stuck in the sand, and bounced back onto the track.

After three or four laps, the oil pressure looked low, and I came in. The crew told me it was fine and sent me back out. I did another few laps, still with low pressure, and came back in. This time, an official ran up to my car waving his arms.

The pit wall was just a stripe of paint on the ground. A drivers' meeting that Bizzarrini hadn't known about had detailed the rules about crossing this line. I'd crossed it the wrong way on each stop, and they disqualified me. Bizzarrini could have protested, but maybe he preferred to go out because of my mistake than the car's imminent failure. My debut at Le Mans was over with 23 hours to go. My main reaction was disappointment that I couldn't keep driving the car. It was in the same class as the Corvette, but it was much faster, very low to the ground, and it handled beautifully.

We were there to watch the finish, as Ford went one-two-three with Ken Miles leading, though in a now-infamous decision, the officials would classify him second because the second-place car on the track had started behind and therefore travelled the greater distance.

The distance between our team and that team was so great that it never occurred to me that this could be my future, that I could be in a position to be one of those guys I was watching.

Can-Am, 1966
McLaren M1B

I met Ray Caldwell in Nassau at the Bahamas Speed Week, at a sort of racing holiday at the end of the season, very amateur and fun — big drinking every night, and the first time you might have to show your face would be 2 p.m. the next day, to get in a lap or two of practice. The track was endless, bumpy, and poorly maintained, but we all loved it.

They had a race for Formula Vees with a huge purse, something like $50,000, that had attracted drivers as illustrious as Bruce McLaren. I was there with my Vee. The cars were all in an old airplane hangar. Ray was the national champion in Formula Vee in a car he'd designed himself. He was funny, full of energy, expansive.

I'd been driving my Porsche 904 in SCCA nationals. Ray and I co-drove it in a 300-mile race at Watkins Glen in the rain and won. Jim Kaser, the head of the SCCA competition department, was promoting a new series for the next season: the Can-Am. The SCCA, more of a gentlemen's club, had a strong bias against professional racing, but the Can-Am would be for pros, with enormous prize money and no real restrictions on what car you could enter. Stirling Moss was the spokesman — he was taking people for rides around Central Park in someone's old Lola. We already knew that Dan Gurney, Bruce McLaren, Chris Amon, John Surtees, and Jim Hall were planning to enter.

Together Ray and I decided that the best next step for me would be the under 2-liter class of the Can-Am. He would design the car. But before we could get started, Bizzarrini

called, on the heels of my drive at Le Mans, offering to give us the open car for the higher class of the Can-Am.

I was living in Marblehead, Massachusetts with Ray and his first wife at the time. We were so excited that I kept my doubts about the competitiveness of the car to myself. Then Bizzarrini called back with one qualification: we had to insure the car. We found out we could buy our own car for the open class for less. While still expensive, the new plan seemed almost reasonable next to the one we'd just been considering.

We had a choice between a McLaren and a Lola chassis, and a Chevy and a Ford engine. Ray reasoned that the McLaren was a space frame and would be easier to fix when I crashed. It was my first indication that Ray might have lacked some confidence in my driving. We chose the Ford because it was more reliable. The best combination turned out to be the Lola and the Chevy.

Ray found a McLaren in Houston, Texas. The chassis and ZF gearbox cost $10,000. The engine, a 289 Ford — the engine that had powered the Le Mans winners — was $3,500. We got a pickup and trailer for $4,000. I painted the car white with a wide blue stripe down the center and put the same stripe on the pickup, along with the A of the logo of Ray's company, Autodynamics, and we were in the Can-Am.

We first drove the car at an SCCA national at Thompson. No one there had ever seen a Can-Am car, and its performance was startling. It was the first time I was ever scared in a car. Some air was leaking under the windshield, and at times I had to hold my helmet on. We won as if no other cars were on the track.

Just a week later was the first ever Can-Am, at St.

Bridgehampton

Jovite. It was mid-morning as we pulled into the paddock, the first practice already underway. John Harkness, an aspiring young driver who was working for us that weekend as a mechanic, went over with me to watch.

At turn one, the cars were turning right at the bottom of a dip, climbing again, and disappearing over a hill. You could tell that Bruce McLaren and Chris Amon were the fastest. John later told me that he took a look at them and knew that this wasn't for him. I just remember wanting to get in my car.

In the next practice, I was cresting the hill in the middle

of the straight and saw a car off the track spinning upside down. I stopped as close as I could and ran over. A group of us tipped the car back on its wheels, gravel raining out of it. The driver, Paul Hawkins, looked back at the track and then at me and then at the track and in his eloquent Australian way said, "Fuck."

I qualified just in front of the McLaren Chevrolet of Charlie Hayes, who had just clinched the SCCA national championship. I got a fair start in the race and was going for eighth place near the end, which would have been a great result for me, not to mention big money, when the battery came loose. I pitted to fix it and wound up in last. John Surtees won with a Lola Chevy.

In the third race, at Mosport, it rained during the first session of qualifying. As at Indy, they had two sessions, and everyone who qualified in the first session started ahead of everyone in the second. It was a dangerous track, and knowing they could make up lost places with relative ease in the race, the top teams didn't go out. With its lower horsepower, our car was easier to drive in the wet. We saw our chance and qualified fifth. When Jerry Grant looked at the scoring tower, he said, "Who the fuck is Sam Posey?"

In the photo of the start, I'm in #33, between the McLarens of Chris Amon and Bruce McLaren; Dan Gurney, who had the pole, is on the inside. In the first turn, four of the top guys crashed. Early on, Mark Donohue was third and I was fourth, and then I broke down. I sat on a berm overlooking the track and watched as the leaders dropped out and Mark won — his first big win and one that helped launch his career.

Afterward, John Surtees, one of the drivers who'd had a bad start, complained that I'd hit him from behind. I knew I hadn't, because he'd started behind me. The next weekend was the grand prix at Watkins Glen; he was in it, and I was watching. By then, a few headlines had appeared about how I'd hit him. I came up to talk to him as he was getting out of his rental car. He stopped me, showed me a picture of the start at Mosport with me ahead of him, and apologized.

After the first three races, Ray and I thought we needed more horsepower. Weber made a side-draft carburetor that seemed like the answer. We bought the only one available. Ray had to go somewhere by plane to get it; he flew back with it sitting in his lap. It never worked, and we didn't finish the last three races. The lesson about the costs of hubris could have served us well the next season — if we'd learned it.

The last photo shows me off to a promising start in the final race at Stardust, before breaking down.

Mosport, Canada

Stardust, Las Vegas

Off to the USRRC
McLaren M1B, 1967

The United States Road Racing Championship was like the Can-Am but an American version, minus Jim Hall, Bruce McLaren, and John Surtees. I'd had the pole and finished second in the first round, at Las Vegas, but followed that result with two DNFs.

Off the start at Bridgehampton, the fourth round, I was back a few places. Impatient, I went boiling down into turn three and lost it. The turn is tricky — a slight downhill into a climbing right. I shifted down before the right and locked up the rear when I got back on the power. I wound up in

Bridgehampton

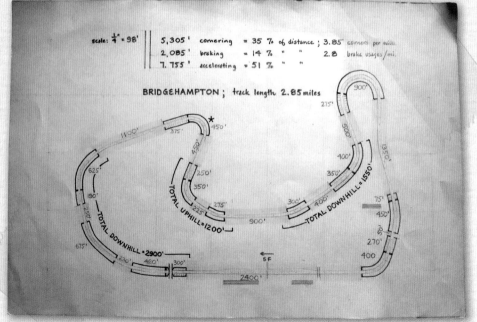

scale: 1/4" = 98'

5,305' cornering = 35 % of distance ; 3.85 corners per mile
2,085' braking = 14 % " " 2.8 brake usages/mi.
7,755' accelerating = 51 % " "

BRIDGEHAMPTON ; track length 2.85 miles

Watkins Glen

Lothar Motschenbacher and Sam Posey both in McLaren-Chevys are about to overtake Fred Baker's Porsche Carrera 6. Motschenbacher, hampered by a loose seat, finished third behind Posey. (John Hearst photos)

Journalistic truth has its place, but it doesn't seem to be the race track. Brock Yates blew the engine in his '67 Dodge Dart, but had an audience.

Mark Donohue was challenged by Sam Posey's McLaren early in the race. Posey got by for one lap but Donohue recovered to win his fourth USRRC race at Watkins Glen.

the dark, half buried in the sand, and had to kick the door open to get out. When we flipped the car back over, it was full of sand but otherwise hardly damaged.

In preparation for the Can-Am season that followed the USRRC, I made a map of each track. Here you see the one for Bridgehampton, with a star marking where I went off.

The start photo shows the next USRRC round, at Watkins Glen, where I was holding second in #2. Soon after, I would pass Mark Donohue — the only driver to do it that season. Too bad it didn't last. In the news cutting, my mom holds my pit board.

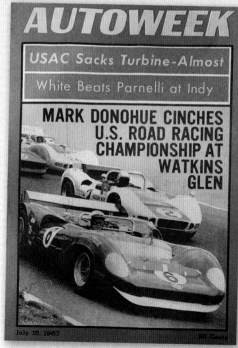

AUTOWEEK

USAC Sacks Turbine-Almost

White Beats Parnelli at Indy

MARK DONOHUE CINCHES U.S. ROAD RACING CHAMPIONSHIP AT WATKINS GLEN

July 15, 1967   35 Cents

Sam Posey's mother assisted the young Sharon, Conn., driver in his quest for victory. Her pit board shows Posey's practice times as he got down to 1:13.9 to qualify second to Mark Donohue, identical to the finishing positions.

Rocky Mountain Man Big Winner At Porsche Parade in Capital

WASHINGTON, D.C., June 23 — Bill Randle of the Rocky Mountain region was the overall winner of the 12th Porsche Parade held here this week.

Competition at the event was divided into a concours, a rally, and a high-speed autocross.

Randle, driving his Road America Carrera roadster, bested some 333 other Porsche enthusiasts. Second overall was Bob Simmons of the Gold Coast region and Don Clever of the Monterey Bay region.

A highlight of the meet was a tech session opened by Porsche of America vice-president O. E. Filius and presided over by general service manager Herbert Dramm.

Dramm reported that all 1968 Porsches will comply with the new

Buzz Hahn of the Gold Coast region won a technical quiz Friday afternoon, involving mechanical details of Porsches.

Among the instructors at a Driver's School Wednesday and Thursday was Bob Tullius. Tullius and other SCCA drivers took the students on three-lap rides around Marlboro, then turned them loose for 30 minutes of observed practice.

The German Embassy here had a reception for the Porsche enthusiasts.

Event chairman Robert S. Lee announced that next year's Parade would be at Palm Beach, Fla., hosted by the Gold Coast region.

Minute barrier
McLaren M1B, Lime Rock, 1967

For years, fast cars had been lapping Lime Rock within three or four seconds of a minute. Excitement built as drivers came closer to the barrier. The local newspapers even reported on the attempts. I would go down into turn one with my stopwatch to see how fast guys were, rooting for someone to break through.

I had been at the track when a team of Scarabs showed up for a national SCCA race in 1960 (pictured). They kept the cars at a garage down the road from our house. I thought their lead driver, Harry Heuer, was primed to break the minute. To count, the time had to occur in a race. In practice, I timed Heuer at 1:04, 1:02, and then a minute flat, and then he pitted. In the race, he never beat that time.

Three years passed before Jim Haynes made his run. He'd had a big engine installed in his Lotus 18. I went to the pits so I could be the first to congratulate him. He stopped right at my feet and shook his head; he'd come close but didn't dare push harder. The barrier almost seemed more solid after surviving such promising challenges.

By 1967, I had my McLaren for the Can-Am. No one had ever brought a car like this to Lime Rock. I probably had 100 hp on Jim's big engine. I scheduled a stop at the Lime Rock nationals in the middle of the USRRC season. About 30 drivers in the field could have broken a minute in my car. I did a 1:01 from a standing start in practice, and then a 56. After the race, people congratulated me with much more enthusiasm than my own part in the achievement deserved. They seemed satisfied to see the barrier fall to such a phenomenal car. I think that lap did more for my prestige at my home track than any other success I had there.

Skip Barber had his own McLaren and went faster by two seconds in September, a couple months later.

in just 30 minutes Sam Posey set a track record and won the English Leather® Lime Trophy at Lime Rock, Connecticut July 4, 1967

Out of our depth
Caldwell D7

At the end of that summer, we finished third in the informal championship of the USRRC. On that wave of momentum, Ray Caldwell and I evolved a plan to build a car that would beat the Chaparral.

Everyone else in the Can-Am was running an independent rear suspension. Ray reasoned that a solid axle would be simpler, stronger, and give us superior traction. You could spin the wheels of those cars in third gear.

I developed the body with Eugene Larrabee, an MIT professor and a friend of Ray's. Larrabee built our own wind tunnel a few feet long out of a hundred soda straws and a fan. As far as I know, we were the only people except Jim Hall to build one. I made the model of the car out of a block of wood. We suspended the model above a little tray on thin wires, the fan blew air through the straws, and they evened out the pressure of the air before it passed over the model. You could measure how much downforce you were getting at the nose and tail by how much the wires compressed,

Ray's shop in Marblehead was an average place but just what we needed. By then I was renting an apartment on the water. I would go to the shop every day, where I had little to do but pay the bills. Sometimes they reached $10,000 in a week; I would feel as if I could hardly breathe.

The first race of the 1967 Can-Am was at Elkhart Lake. When Bruce McLaren saw our car in the pits, he accused us of copying his nose. We hadn't, but they were almost identical. Our big rear wing looked like the Chaparral's.

We were almost a second up on everyone else in the carousel. We knew we had something. But everywhere else we were hopeless. Something was off in the steering geometry. The nose lurched from side to side, sometimes up to a yard. On the straights, it didn't matter much, but in the turns, you couldn't attack an entry, apex, or exit without fear of going off.

People thought we were romantics, fighting the juggernauts. But we were so naive we didn't really know what we were up against. To us, each step in the design had seemed like a logical next step. It was only as the project came together that I saw our naivete as it must have appeared to others.

Ray had designed our wheels himself; he thought we could save some weight, and they could change to accommodate tires with different sidewall heights. We thought maybe they were contributing to the lurches.

The uprights of the Chaparral wing pressed down on the suspension, ours on the body, so their downforce went directly to the tires, while ours had to go through the suspension. Their wing got more grip, although it was always breaking.

After Elkhart Lake came Bridgehampton, a track that emphasized handling. We did no better there.

drag by how much the pan pushed back as the air passed over the car. With a slight difference in the angle at the nose, the drag went way up. Not exactly today's Formula One technology, but I believe the aerodynamics of the body were respectable for the time. It was the one part of the car we wouldn't later try to change.

Elkhart Lake

My worst crash
Lime Rock, 1967

After the Can-Am at Mosport, halfway through the 1967 season, we went to Lime Rock — where I'd broken the minute that summer — for a test. The Caldwell car had shown flashes of potential overshadowed by serious flaws. We had no sponsors. All the expenses were coming out of my pocket.

We tried taking off the wing, replacing it with a piece of masonite taped to the back of the car like a spoiler sticking up a couple inches above the rear deck. After a lap or two, I was two seconds faster.

On the next lap, confident it was going to be the best yet, I was hurtling toward the uphill turn when something snapped in the left front suspension and jammed under the nose of the car, throwing it up into the air. It landed on an embankment that served as a guardrail on the exit.

Butch Sherwood, the track manager, later found rivets from the car in oak trees beside the track, 20 feet up. I still remember a vivid image of the clear blue of the sky between the front fenders as the car took off — then, like the next shot in a slideshow, some trees with silvery leaves. The great John Morton later doubted this part of my account, but I stand by it!

I came to in the car, upside down. The car had dug into the ground. It was as if I was looking up from the bottom of a well; I felt I had to strain to get up to the light, which I guess was the feeling of coming to.

Since it was a test day, no course workers were around.

No one else had been on the track with me. It was quiet except for the ticking of the fuel pumps. The switches were right near my face, but in my daze I didn't grasp that since the pumps both had to be on, turning them off meant flipping both switches in the other direction. I reversed only one, to reduce a potential fire by half. I had always had a terror of fire. My right foot was stuck in the pedals. I decided that if a fire started, I would break my right ankle with my left foot and then crawl away as far and fast as possible.

But then a few moments passed and nothing happened.

With a twist, my foot came free. One of the fuel tanks was now above me, pressing on my chest. I moved my head in the dirt to get a little more space. As I started worming my way out, the car shifted a little, the tank pressing down again, but not enough to trap me.

After I got out, still dazed, I wandered around in the woods for half an hour. The car was completely out of sight, and in the pits, Ray and our chief mechanic, Jack McCormack, had no idea where I'd gone. Finally, I came out on the track around where I'd left it. By then, someone

I knew was lapping in his Lotus Seven. He saw me on the bank and picked me up.

A little after I got back to the pits, he told me to take the Lotus out for a few laps, to shake off the crash. All I remember was the tachometer, electric and rectangular. In my first flying lap, I set a new record for the class.

Ray seemed more inclined to explain the crash through driver error than design failure. I knew that the front suspension had failed. We went out to the turn, and I found a long gash in the track surface where a piece of the suspension had dug in.

Back in the pits, Ray and I talked over what to do. We had a second chassis in the Marblehead shop and a few days to turn it into a car before the next race. Mike Goth, another Can-Am driver, had run out of money — a frequent occurrence in the Can-Am — and was selling his car, a Lola. By then the Lola looked like a better car than the McLaren —

Riverside

Restored Caldwell at Lime Rock

faster and also safer, which had come to mean more to me.

With the factor of the car held constant, I would have had a chance to prove myself as a driver. I should have bought the Lola and driven it with all I had; I think I could have been fourth or fifth in most of the races. But the lap before the crash, our car was the best it had ever been. I couldn't give up on the project quite yet.

The next Can-Am was at Laguna Seca. The car arrived late, we didn't practice much, and I started at the back. I had to pit on the first lap with a misfire. When I came out, the track was empty in front of me. I was furious — at the misfire, at a sense that I was making a series of bad decisions. My time for that lap equaled one that Bruce McLaren did later for the lap record.

Lola, Bridgehampton, 1968
Rodriguez following

Between Laguna and the next round, at Riverside, we took the Caldwell to Troutman and Barnes, who'd built the Scarabs that Harry Heuer had driven at Lime Rock. They designed and built an elegant replacement for our masonite spoiler — the two little fins you can see at the back — that also directed the air through the adjacent oil coolers.

But the other problems with the car persisted. In the end, our best moment of the season came at the closing banquet, when Bruce McLaren presented us with an award for the greatest innovation in design. He gave me a real handshake and the impression that he admired what we'd done with very little resources and maybe less knowledge. I was gratified, though we'd spent quite a bit for that award.

In 1968, Brett Lunger joined our team. He was a DuPont heir and a marine. When a professor at Princeton had suggested that the best way to understand the conflict in Vietnam was to experience it, Brett had volunteered for a five-year tour. By 1968, he'd finished his three years of active duty but still had to go to a training camp every two weeks — an inconvenience to the start of his racing career. Challenged one night after dinner, he did 25 one-armed push-ups in the parking lot.

He bought a Lola T160. By the second race of the season, at Bridgehampton, it was clear that he had the better car. He came up to me and said, "It won't make a difference to anyone if I finish 15th or 20th, but it will make a big difference if you're in the top five or not." He switched cars with me for the rest of the season. In the next race, I finished fourth.

Charlie Fox
Test at VIR

We'd done the Can-Am for three years, proven we couldn't beat the top guys, and couldn't afford it anymore. We were at Virginia International Raceway with Brett Lunger's Lola T160, the best car I'd driven to that date, to turn it over to its new owner, who planned to hire a few mechanics and go race the Can-Am, just as we had done.

The writer Charles Fox was there to drive the car for an article for *Car & Driver* before the new owner took it.

I warmed the car up, and Charlie got in and did a lap or two. He came in, and we told him to take it up to whatever speed felt comfortable. The track was damp, except for under the spectator bridge. When he came out from the bridge and hit the wet, he was accelerating hard with the car's 650 hp. The car kicked out on him and spun off into the woods going backwards. Something caught the fuel tank and bent it out away from the body, but it didn't catch fire. A sapling wound

up jammed against Charlie's thigh; we had to cut it out to get him loose.

Charlie was okay. His magazine's insurance would reimburse the new owner. But I could tell the wreck was hard on Jack McCormack, our chief mechanic. He'd done so much work on the car, and it was perfect. As far as I know, the new owner didn't end up racing the Can-Am; maybe he was discouraged by the effort to find another car, or the sight of the wreck. Charlie's article, which came out a few weeks later, was good as anything I'd read about car racing.

LeGrand not so grand
Formula 5000, 1968

I'd accepted a ride at Mosport to drive an unusual Formula 5000 car called the LeGrand. The car was very fast, but the suspension looked too flimsy to last a race. I was cautious in qualifying but had the best time. I told the car owner, Pete Botsford, that I would drive one lap of the race so he could collect the starting money. I was happy with the deal because I could see myself in a photo on the cover of the next *Autoweek* leading the pack.

This photo shows me leading into the first turn. The car was so fast that I had my feet on the ground in the pits before the second car crossed the start/finish. In their cover shot, to include the rest of the field, *Autoweek* cropped me out. The suspension collapsed on the sister car halfway through the race, and the driver, Jack Eiteljorg, was severely injured.

A year earlier, I would have accepted the ride and hoped for the best. That weekend made me think I could make more mature decisions.

Penske driver
Trans-Am, 1968

In the 1968 Trans-Am season, Mark Donohue's chief rivals were Parnelli Jones and George Follmer. Donohue was driving for Roger Penske, the top Camaro team, and Jones and Follmer were in the Mustangs of Bud Moore. Roger worried that Parnelli and George would gang up on Mark. Midway through the season, with Mark leading the championship, Roger offered me a ride as Mark's teammate for the next four races. I had to pay for it, but with Penske's reputation well established by then, I knew what a chance it was.

In the first race, I crashed in practice. As the first photo shows, the car was in bad shape. Roger sent his Learjet to his headquarters near Philadelphia to bring back the spare parts. His crew worked through the night and repaired the car. I finished third in that race and the next two — good results, but not great. I had the feeling the team thought I would do better.

At Watkins Glen, Mark was sick and couldn't drive. Our chances of a win — and keeping Follmer and Jones out of the points — rested with me. I was leading near the end when Rusty Jowett crashed at the top of the uphill; when I came past, I ran over some debris and flatspotted the left front tire.

The car began shaking so badly that I thought I might not make it to the finish. I'd once heard Roger say that if something was wrong with the car, fix it right away and get back on the attack. He was a perfectionist who didn't like to see his cars on the track in anything but the best condition. I came in. They fixed the car, and I finished second behind Jerry Titus.

Afterward, Roger wouldn't speak to me. As he saw it, I'd thrown away the win. I never got a chance to explain that

I'd done what I thought he would have. He didn't extend my contract through the end of the season. As it turned out, he would never hire me again, but I still thought the experience had been worth it.

At the start of the next year, I went to the Daytona 24 hours hoping I might get to drive with Mark. But someone bought the ride for Chuck Parsons. Discouraged, I was wandering around the garages when my PR man, Ron Meade, suggested I go see Luigi Chinetti's team; they seemed to have a lot of Ferraris.

Dick Fritz was the team manager. He asked me to take a car around to the pits. It was a stock GTB, beige. When I got out, he said I'd done a nice job with the drive and offered me a ride. Out of the loss of one race with Roger — a rare race they didn't win — came four years at Le Mans with Chinetti and Ferrari.

In Parnelli's dust
Baja, 1968

The Baja is a 1000-mile off-road race in Mexico, starting just below the California border. In the early years, about 20 miles were paved. Most of the racers — or those who made their way down the peninsula; very few actually raced — were lovers of adventure, dreamers setting off with no chance of finishing, let alone winning.

I believe the race gained much of its renown from the participation of Parnelli Jones. He was charismatic and perfectly suited to the challenge — rough and tough, and with outright skill that few if any could approach. He won the 1000-miler twice by great margins.

A few weeks before the 1968 Baja, I received an invitation from a group of young mechanics in San Francisco to drive a car they called a Peccari. As far as I know, they just figured I was an adventurous guy who would make the most of the opportunity. They treated me like a champ. I probably never entered another race in which I was less equipped for the challenges ahead.

The Baja took place between the Can-Am at Riverside and the next one, two weeks later, at Stardust in Las Vegas. Calculating the required time to finish based on Parnelli's, I had no fear that I wouldn't be back in time.

I first met with the team and the car in San Francisco. The car was a homebuilt contraption with a VW engine and transmission, slab sides, and a giant wing on the top, which wouldn't have been effective at under 80 mph. The builders were going on nothing but a certain romantic idea of the

race, and I was as clueless as they were. Ignorance was bliss.

The team chartered a small plane for me over the course so I could see what lay ahead. I was fascinated. I loved the desert, and this was the desert of deserts. The course was nothing but a slight rut in some places where people had practiced. You could make a wrong turn around a cactus and never find your way back. We had a map, and the towns that were checkpoints along the way — more like collections of huts — were easy enough to spot from the air that we could be fairly certain we were in fact over the course.

The night before the race, I met the team in Ensenada, on the Mexican side of the border. The race started just after dawn, the cars going off one at a time, the order determined by class and likely finishing time, with the faster cars starting later. A couple hundred entrants had lined up: mostly motorcycles and modified dune buggies like ours. We were somewhere near the back.

Ensenada

One of the builders was my co-driver. We pulled forward until they waved us onto the course. The first section, at sea level, was paved. We turned off that onto a dirt road, which was still okay. Then came the first real desert section.

The obstacles included boulders, cacti, and arroyos, which were ditches a few car lengths long. The Mexicans would hide behind some bushes near these arroyos to enjoy the spectacle of your disaster without tipping you off to it in advance.

Within a few miles, it became clear that the car was about as unsuited to the demands of the race as I was. The team had lengthened the gear ratio over the stock version, thinking we would be charging along at Parnelli's speed, but we couldn't break 30. The giant wing on the roof was the most visible proof of the laughable gap between our illusions and reality. Every single foot of the way was perilous, even at the slow speed — or maybe because of it; Parnelli was floating over some of the obstacles that threatened to flip us. Within the first ten miles, he overtook us in a blaze of sand and glory, looking like he was doing 200.

Conditions deteriorated as night came on. Cacti taller than our wing seemed to jump into our path with arms raised in alarm. At one of the outposts along the route, we gave up. I don't think we'd made it a hundred miles.

Sometime in the daylight, a truck picked me up. I'm not sure where it had come from, but it was transporting a load of turtles back toward Ensenada. I rode with them in the back. John Wayne's son also happened to be aboard, up in the cab.

I made it to Las Vegas in time for the Can-Am. When I went for my wallet at the hotel reception, sand spilled onto the desk.

Pretty, slow
Sebring, 1969

This was my second drive for Luigi Chinetti, at Sebring. My Ferrari Dino 206 GT, shared with Bob Dini, was the slowest car on the track. But it was fun to drive, the numbers were pretty, and when the race was over, someone came up to us and told us we'd won our class.

Steve Allen's Classic Wax Special
Formula 5000, 1969

Here I am with Steve Allen, the first host of *The Tonight Show*. His wife and her sister, Jane and Audrey Meadows, were the daughters of a preacher from my hometown. Before the 1969 Formula 5000 season, I wrote him a letter with this information and a request to use his name in connection with our sponsor, which I thought would help us land the sponsor. He agreed, and the Eagle we'd bought from Dan Gurney became Steve Allen's Classic Wax Special. He even invited me to appear on his show along with the car — squeezing into it himself, driving around the block outside the studio on Sunset Boulevard, and crashing onto the stage through a wall of cardboard bricks.

After the Can-Am, everything seemed like a bargain in Formula 5000. We couldn't spend enough on the Eagle. Before the 1969 season, Jack McCormack worked on it all winter, and it was immaculate.

Ron Courtney
Riverside, 1969

The first Formula 5000 race of 1969 was at Riverside. After the fifth lap of qualifying, I had the pole and a new record for the class. On the sixth lap, I was coming up to turn six, a third-gear left-hander on the downslope of a hill. We were experimenting with some Airhart brakes. They were very light, but as I came up the hill, the pedal went to the floor.

I reached the turn-in point at the crest of the hill going around 140 mph. A yellow car was sideways across the track around the apex of the turn. The spectators were on the right, so I didn't want to go that way. Later I would have to try to work out exactly what I did and why, but I can't really say.

I spun around and hit the car side-on with the back of my car. The other car tripped mine, and I flipped and landed upside down. I came to with flames around me. It turned out they were from gas from the other car that had splashed onto mine. The course workers ran over to me, flipped my car over, and pulled me out. I started running over to the other car. It was more of a gesture; the fire was consuming the car, and I wouldn't have run into it. At any rate, a course worker tackled me on the way.

The other driver was Ron Courtney. He'd spun in the same arc as I had and wound up near the edge of the road. When the course workers tried to push him off the track, he'd put the brakes on. One of the tires half buried at the apex of the turn, to discourage cutting it, was right in front

of him; maybe he hadn't wanted to break his car's nose. By the time they got him out of the car, he had burns all over his body. I should have gone to the hospital to see him, but I was afraid if I did, it would look like an admission of guilt. I've never seen him since.

Exactly a year later, I was sitting on the grid for the Trans-Am at Laguna, and someone came up and put some papers through the window. Belted in, I couldn't reach them. The race was about to start. The papers were still there at the finish. They were the notice that Ron Courtney was suing me.

Courtney's mother was a lawyer, and she managed to enlist F. Lee Bailey, a prosecutor well known at the time for winning a number of large and surprising settlements in automotive cases. Courtney had also sued the track, Firestone tires, the SCCA, Bell Helmets, and Bill Simpson, whose company made Courtney's gloves, shoes, and driving suit.

Courtney's case had weaknesses. Firestone sold a foam insert for our gas tanks to limit explosions, but Courtney hadn't bought one. He'd kept the course workers from pushing him off the track.

His lawyers claimed I'd disregarded the yellow flag at the entrance to the turn. If it was waving, I never saw it. The course workers had a station on some raised ground on the outside of the turn. One of them was filming the track. He captured Courtney's spin and the first waving of the flag. The camera went off before the crash. But before it went off, the flag was no longer waving. I had been just in front of Courtney when he spun. I argued that they must have grown tired of waving the flag by the time I came back around.

The case dragged on for over a year. Almost every day, I had a moment of terror of losing. It would have been the end of my career and more. Finally, my friend John Whitman met with our lawyers and Courtney's. I was in a cottage in a boatyard in Florida when John called me. I remember that I was standing in front of the refrigerator, my then-girlfriend Ellen behind me. I owed Courtney $25,000 — a staggering sum on its face, but Bailey had been settling cases for $5 million.

THE NEW YORK TIMES, SUNDAY, JULY 11, 1976

VIEWS OF SPORT

In Auto Racing, Accidents Are No-Fault Collisions. Sometimes

Sam Posey will be driving a Formula 5000 car at Watkins Glen today. This harrowing story of his crash in a Can-Am Eagle at Riverside, Calif., in April 1969 is adapted from the book "The Mudge Pond Express," by Sam Posey, published by G. P. Putnam's Sons. ©1976 by Sam Posey.

By SAM POSEY

I brought the Eagle out of Turn Six, a 160-degree right hand turn, and accelerated down the undulating straight toward Turn Seven, which was a fairly slow lefthander. The approach to Turn Seven was sharply uphill, and from the car the turn itself was invisible behind the hill.

As I entered the braking zone I pushed the brake pedal—and it went right to the floor. I tried to pump the pedal, but it stayed on the floor. No brakes! I was going 140 miles an hour.

The spectators were on my right; Turn Seven would be coming up to my left.

I twisted the wheel to the left, purposely provoking a high-speed spin just as the car swept up the hill toward the turn. At that instant I had a flash of what was about to happen: I would spin through the turn, off the far side of the track and into the bank. Spinning the car would reduce the speed of impact, but it would still be a serious crash. "The car is going to take a beating in this one," I thought as I hurtled over the crest of the hill.

And then grim anticipation gave way to horror as I saw what had not been visible from the straightaway: another car sitting sideways in the middle of the road, directly in my path. Dark blue, with chrome sparkling in the sun.

I felt my car going backward in its spin. Then I was into the other car with a terrific collision, my engine and gearbox tearing into the soft fuel tanks like a battering ram. A mighty wrenching-free—flight—my front wheels silhouetted against the sky—my car starting to roll over in midair—an explosion of flame far below me. Now I was upside down and falling; the road came up to meet me.

My car landed upside down, slid off into the dirt and stopped. It was bright in the cockpit. The rollbar had held up and I could see out between the ground and the edge of the cockpit.

People's feet appeared in my little window. They lifted the car enough for me to wriggle out. There was smoke everywhere and people running—my God!

The other car—the driver's still in it—I've got to get him out! I started toward the car, which was bent in the middle like a splintered branch. Someone grabbed my arm and spun me around. I was looking into the anguished face of one of the corner workers.

"He's trapped! Can't you see that?" he shouted. "We're going to have to cut him out of the car."

They led me over to the side of the road. Suddenly, very dizzy, I sat down. A little later, someone handed me a cup of water.

"How is he?" I asked.

"I don't know. They think he's still alive."

The other driver's name was Ron Courtney. There was nothing I could do to help him. And as I went back over the sequence of the crash—the pedal going to the floor, my decision to pump the brakes, my decision to pitch the car into a spin with a trajectory away from the spectators—I knew that I had acted under extreme pressure exactly as I would have if there had been time to deliberate every maneuver. Presently, the wreckers came to remove the shattered cars. As I watched the remains of the Eagle being hoisted off the ground, it occurred to me to be thankful for the way it had held up in the crash. It was inherently a strong car, but during the winter it had been made even safer by installation of a heavier rollbar and an automatic fire-fighting system; that extra insurance had probably saved my life.

I couldn't sleep that night. My mind was used to shutting out disappointments—this was something new. I watched all the late movies and then sat outside on the steps in the cool night leaning back against the door. I knew that 300 miles to the south, in Riverside, Ron Courtney was still on the critical list and was fighting for his life. I tried to make sense out of the extremes of horror and ecstasy that had been encompassed in the last two weeks, but they were as sounds that are beyond the range of human hearing.

To my unspeakable relief, Ron Courtney lived through his ordeal. Then he sued me. Me, and almost every other individual and company that had been even remotely involved in the accident.

I had never heard of one driver suing another for something that happened on the track; for as long as racing has existed, the participants have recognized that it is a dangerous activity and that those who race do so at their own peril. Indeed, every driver must sign a waiver of liability to that effect before he is allowed on the track. But did precedent mean anything? I didn't know anything about law. All I knew was that Courtney had retained as his lawyer the famous Melvin Belli.

In the first weeks after I was sued, I struggled with a bewildering morass of lawyers and depositions. The initial assumption was that I would be covered by the Sports Car Club of America master insurance plan, but on closer inspection it was discovered that the policy did not apply to driver-versus-driver lawsuits. I was on my own.

Fans and racing people from all over the country wrote to me to express their indignation at what Courtney had done. At first I was indignant, too, and bitter. As a driver I had done all the right things in the car, and yet I was being victimized by this lawsuit.

But slowly I began to understand the situation from Courtney's perspective. Frightfully injured, hospitalized for months, medical bills exhausting his financial resources, at some point he must have wanted to lash out in any direction that might produce some money for him and his family.

Four years 11 months after the complaint was served on me, the lawsuit was settled out of court. Throughout all that time it took only a week, or a phrase, or some idle thought in the middle of the night to bring the dull dread of the suit to the front of my mind, and to recall the horror of the day it represented.

Rich George

Mailbox: Olympic Picks

Battle of the Sexes

To the Sports Editor:

The selection process of the United States Olympic team has recently come

To the Sports Editor:

Let the Best Machine Win? Precisely, No

By STEVE FELDBERG

official becomes fierce. One wrong call and his veracity has been destroyed for the rest of the game. And, knowing the nected by wire to a computer terminal. This terminal, upon the exertion of pressure by the swimmer on the pad at the against each other while recording these times, hardly anyone could have detect-

A low and a high
Formula 5000, Laguna Seca, May 1969

The Courtney crash was an inauspicious beginning to the 1969 season, but I never thought of pulling out. Right after the crash, I started looking for a new car. I found one for sale right there in pit lane. It was a brownish purple with white-lace highlights — a discouraging contrast to the perfect car I'd just wrecked. But it was an Eagle, with an engine and some spares for the transmission. The owner was asking $10,000. We couldn't have bought a set of wheels for that much in the Can-Am.

The next race was a week away at Laguna Seca. We could transport the car there on our trailer, avoiding the hassles of shipping. In three days, Jack managed to prepare the car. He even repainted it in our colors. I won the race. For me, the first two races of 1969 would represent the highs and lows of Formula 5000.

In 1969, for the first time, the series offered enough prize money to be an attraction. On paper, the season looked like a battle between us and Tony Adamowicz, but you wouldn't

Sam Posey shows a winner's smile to Royal 76-Continental Championship queen Norma Foster after capturing the second event in the Formula A series, May 4. (John Dickerson photo)

know it from watching the races. Tony had a car with a very reliable engine; for the same reason, he wasn't as fast. We almost never raced wheel to wheel. And one of the season's decisive moments came off the track.

Going into Elkhart Lake, the sixth round, Jack McCormack had been making steady improvements to the car, and now it was perfect. Ron Morse, our mechanic, was taking the car to Wisconsin from LA with my friend John Whitman. They had delayed setting out as long as possible to allow for some last work on the car. It was a long haul. Somewhere in Arizona, Ron fell asleep at the wheel. The trailer went down end over end into a valley of rocks. John fractured a bone in his neck; he's never been able to turn his head all the way to one side since. But in a miracle, this was the worst injury they suffered. My car, however, was totaled. Elkhart Lake was a double 500. Tony won both races.

Showdown
Formula 5000, 1969, final rounds

With over half the season to go, we still had time to mount a comeback, but we needed yet another car. Technical changes were coming so fast that the McLaren M10A was now the car of choice. I bought one. I won at Lime Rock. At Sears Point, John Cannon short-braked me, and I hit him and went out.

Meanwhile, David Hobbs had entered the series mid-season, coming over from Europe. He started racking up points immediately, so many that he too was in contention going into the last race, at Sebring.

On our trip down to Florida, we stopped to test at a track in Georgia. I broke the lap record. The owner was thrilled and went off in search of some trophy to commemorate the achievement. He returned with a toilet seat inscribed with the record.

It all came down to a blustery day at Sebring early in December. With a good finish, I would win the championship. I got off to a bad start, stuck down in fifth or sixth. Hobbs, the wildcard, was likely to win. I knew I had to move up. I was following Cannon when he short-braked me again. I ran into a 50-gallon drum placed at the edge of the track.

Tony Adamowicz won the championship by two points from David. I was third.

Brainerd, Minnesota

Tony A to Z

Sebring

Shelby Mustang
Trans-Am, Lime Rock, May 1969

I was chatting with Peter Revson at Indy just after he'd qualified and I hadn't. The race was a conflict with the Trans-Am at Lime Rock, where he was supposed to drive for Carroll Shelby, and he suggested I call about the ride. Lew Spencer, Shelby's right-hand man, took the call. I heard him shouting across the hallway to Shelby, who asked who the hell Sam Posey was. Lew did my bio a good service, and Carroll shouted back, "How much does he want?" I said $5,000, the first number that came to mind — I had paid Roger Penske $4,000 a race the year before — and Shelby agreed.

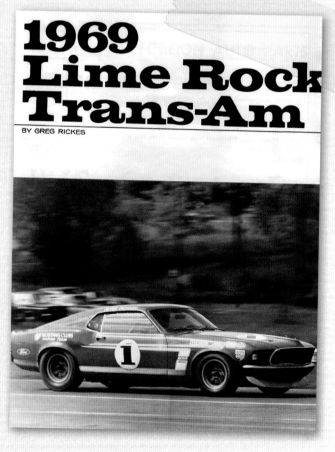

1969 Lime Rock Trans-Am

BY GREG RICKES

Sam Posey of Sharon after he drove to victory in the 1969 Schaefer Trans-Am at Lime Rock. (Photo by Mike Sharin-Lou Marra)

My teammate was Horst Kwech. He'd won the Trans-Am at Riverside for Shelby the year before, but Lime Rock was my home track, and I was determined to be on the pole. With time running out in qualifying, Horst had it. The lap builds through the last three turns at Lime Rock, ending with the downhill, the fastest. I knew I hadn't quite given it everything yet. On that lap, I did, putting two wheels off on the exit. It was enough for the pole by a few tenths.

In the race, Horst took the lead and pulled away, but he broke down. I was leading Swede Savage and John Cannon. With a few laps to go, I lost a cylinder. I backed off, panicked that the engine would blow. Swede appeared in my mirrors, and I tried to think how to block him for more than a lap. But the next lap, he wasn't there; he'd cut a tire. Afterward, the crew had to help me out of the car. The race had lasted over three hours. It would turn out to be the only win for Carroll Shelby that year, and also his last.

Le Mans 24 Hours, 1969
Ferrari 250 LM

I have a strong memory of the gearshift. The car was right-hand drive, the gearlever on the left. The lever was heavy and had momentum when you shifted. The throw was long as you crossed the H. The knob had masking tape covering it to make it less slippery, an heirloom from Jochen Rindt and Masten Gregory. They'd won Le Mans four years earlier with this car, but the NART guys were unsentimental about it. Every time I went from second to third, the lever made a terrible sound. In the first laps of practice, I thought the car wouldn't last more than an hour. The mechanics said Rindt and Gregory had noted the sound too.

What makes Le Mans special? Maybe the length of the race, the history, the foreign country, the size of the grandstand, the sun sliding slowly across a distant field where the Wright Brothers flew, the Mulsanne going on and on forever. In my first finish at Le Mans, in eighth place, I cried when I came around on the last lap and saw all the signal flags waving.

Duel with Dan Gurney
Four-wheel-drive Lotus, Seattle, 1969

The Caldwell might not have succeeded in the way Ray and I had hoped, but it brought us to the attention of people on the scene. One of the most important was a man we didn't know then, Pete Hutchinson, who was working for Chrysler and also writing for *Car and Driver*. Pete assigned himself the story of how we built the car and came out to Marblehead to visit our shop. During the visit, he revealed that his grandfather was president of Chrysler. Soon after, he quit his writing job and became head of Chrysler's racing division.

In 1968, a Lotus with a turbine engine had been leading Indy when it broke down in the last ten laps. For the next year, USAC banned the turbines. After Indy, Chrysler bought the Lotuses and fitted them with stock-block Plymouths to run them for the rest of the season.

Many of these races were on road courses. The team had Joe Leonard driving, but he wasn't a road racer, and the car was not for him. Pete Hutchinson intervened on my behalf. I got in the Lotus for a test at Indy Raceway Park, a road course a few miles from the Speedway.

Andy Granatelli's brother and sidekick, Vince, met me there. Firestone was sponsoring the team, and he said I had better change out of my Goodyear suit and into one of his that said Firestone. I had barely struggled into the bottom half of it when I looked up to see Vince and the other guys laughing at the trailer door. The suit had Mario Andretti's name on it; Mario was a little slimmer than I was.

On the track, I went up to about six-tenths, trying to get a feel for the car. I edged it up to seven-tenths and spun out. I came back into the pits and said I had no idea what had happened. They said I must just be getting used to the car and sent me back out. A lap later, I spun out again in the same spot. I was lucky that the turn had no barriers around it, just a big grassy runoff.

That time I figured it out. The car had four-wheel drive, with a torque split of 40/60 — perfect for Indy, but here, as soon as the tail came out and I tried to correct into the slide, the car followed the front wheels off the track. I think the crew was impressed that I'd diagnosed the problem, and I was pleased: for once, like Donohue, I'd had a technical insight.

It was easy for them to adjust the split. We tried 30/70, and it was a little better, but the car still had the disconcerting tendency to shoot off the road. By then, we'd run out of time to work on it.

Joe Leonard had stuck around for the day of the test. We went out for dinner that night and consumed a good deal of liquor. Joe received the check and was alarmed at the amount. The Chrysler representative told him to take a closer look. It was his Indy qualifying speed, 171 mph.

After the test, the team signed me for the USAC championship. We raced in Seattle, and I had the best race of my life, beating none other than Dan Gurney. The track had no turn with the particular characteristics that had triggered my spins in testing. It was raining, and I had

Gurney on the inside

Max Dudley in his Gerhardt-Chevy (61) leads Mike Mosley, Watson-Turbo-Offy (90) and Billy Vukovich (98), at the rain-swept Dan Gurney 200. Vukovich had difficulty with traction and spun several times. Mosley finished sixth overall.
(Roy Urban photo)

Dan Gurney in his Olsonite Eagle-Ford (48) pulls up on Sam Posey in the STP-sponsored Lotus-Plymouth at the Dan Gurney 200 held in a Washington State rain storm. Posey's car was equipped with a three-speed Torqueflite transmission built by B&M, noted southern California automatic transmission builder.
(Roy Urban photo)

More on:
Sam Posey's Plymouth Takes Dan Gurney For Third Place

(Continued from page 13)

With Unser 35 seconds up on Gurney by lap 10, Andretti was right behind Posey despite the dry tires. Posey, about to pass Gurney down the main straight, spun on the next lap letting Andretti by. Andretti then nipped Gurney for good on lap 13 going into turn one.

At the halfway mark, Posey caught and passed Gurney making the order Unser, by 53 seconds; Andretti, Posey, Gurney, Cannon, Bobby Unser, Hansen, Savage, Mosley and Follmer.

Unser kept pulling away until just five laps to go when he began to slow to finish safely by .66 seconds. Posey was 20 seconds behind Andretti with the final order behind, Gurney, Bobby Unser, after a great comeback; Follmer, Savage, Hansen and Mosley.

The victory for Al gives him nine championship wins against his older brother Bobby's 10. Andretti's chief mechanic, Clint Brawner, celebrated his 50th USAC victory in the first heat, more than any other USAC mechanic.

Ironically, the race's namesake, Gurney, predicted the winner. Between heats when seeing the tire decisions and knowing the Pacific Northwest weather, Gurney told Unser that he would win it all.

DAN GURNEY 200 USAC CHAMPIONSHIP CAR RACE
HEAT ONE: 1 - Mario Andretti, STP Oil Treatment Special Ford, 45 laps or 101.25 miles in 1.09:00 for an average speed of 88.02mph; 2 - Al Unser, Vel's Parnelli Jones Ford, 45 laps; 3 - Dan Gurney, Olsonite Eagle-Ford; 4 - Sam Posey, STP Special Plymouth; 5 - John Cannon, Bryant Heating and Cooling Special Turbo-Ford; 6 - Mike Mosley, Zecol Lubaid Special Turbo-Offy; 7 - Jerry Hansen, Wynn's Pacesetter Homes Ford; 8 - Ludwig Heimrath, Eisert Special Chevy; 9 - Bill Vukovich, Wagner Lockheed Brake Fluid Special Chevy; 10 - Max Dudley, Dudley Trucking Co. Special Chevy; 11 - Bob Gregg, Gregg Enterprise Special Chevy; 12 - Steve Krisiloff, V.T.M. Finishing Corp. Special Ford; 13 - Jerry Grant, Webster Racing Enterprises Special Chevy; 14 - Swede Savage, Olsonite Eagle-Gurney Ford; 15 - George Follmer, Follmer Special Chevy.
DNF: 16 - Art Pollard, STP Special Plymouth, 11 laps, spun and body damage; 17 - Mark Donohue, Sunoco-Simoniz Special Lola-Chevy, 11 laps, bent rear suspension; 18 - Bobby Unser, Bardahl Special Chevy, 11 laps, spun off course; 19 - Johnny Rutherford, Patrick Petroleum Eagle-Ford, 2 laps, broken front suspension.
HEAT TWO: 1 - Al Unser, 45 laps or 101.25 miles in 1.13:00 for an average speed of 83.196mph; 2 - Andretti, 45 laps; 3 - Posey; 4 - Gurney; 5 - B. Unser; 6 - Follmer; 7 - Savage; 8 - Hansen; 9 - Mosley; 10 - Cannon; 11 - Grant; 12 - Pollard; 13 - Heimrath; 14 - Dudley; 15 - Krisiloff; 16 - Gregg.
DNF: 17 - Vukovich, 11 laps, mechanical.
OVERALL (unofficial): 1 - Al Unser; 2 - Andretti; 3 - Posey; 4 - Gurney; 5 - Hansen; 6 - Mosley; 7 - Cannon; 8 - Follmer; 9 - Savage; 10 - Heimrath; 11 - Bobby Unser; 12 - Grant; 13 - Dudley; 14 - Vukovich; 15 - Krisiloff; 16 - Gregg; 17 - Pollard; 18 - Donohue; 19 - Rutherford.

Following
Max Dudley (61)

gracious enough to relive our "duel" many times afterward.

After Seattle, we had one race left, at Riverside. Before the race, we were going to test what Vince thought was a great new idea he'd had for the car. He called me from their shop in Los Angeles just as I was about to board the plane. "I'm glad I caught you," he said. "Stay there." While experimenting again with the torque split, they'd tried putting all the power to the wheels on one side of the car, instead of to the front or the rears, to see whether they could improve cornering in one direction. They'd crashed in the alley behind their shop during the initial test.

They fixed the car for the race. At their home track, they also fielded a second car, signing George Follmer to drive it. I couldn't get within two seconds of him in qualifying. I started the race in midfield and never saw him after the first lap. But I was still living in the glow of having "beaten" Dan Gurney.

Years later, I received a call from Andy Granatelli, the first time I'd heard from him in 20 years. We only talked for a few minutes; he said some gratifying words about our brief association and hung up. A few days later, I learned he'd died.

Firestone tires, which were the best in the rain, and the four-wheel drive for even more stability. Dan had Goodyears and rear-wheel drive. I spent much of the time behind him, watching him work all his magic to control an uncontrollable car. I passed him just before the finish, for third place, so I didn't have to watch out for him behind me. Dan was

GENTLEMEN, START YOUR WINDMILLS

A band of Quixotic malcontents (Sam Posey, Andy Granatelli and Pete Hutchinson) confounded USAC by persisting in the development of their destined-to-be-banned 4-wheel-drive car.

By Sam Posey

Andy Granatelli came toward me, easing his way through the jumble of trailers and station wagons and rent-a-cars parked behind the pit wall at Indianapolis Raceway Park. "Hello," he said. "I'm Andy Granatelli." He spoke with the mixed self-consciousness and assured pride of one who is genuinely famous and knows very well that you know who he is. He studied my Goodyear driving suit with disapproval, eyes glinting ominously under their fleshy lids. "I've got an STP driving suit I'd like you to wear," he growled, raised an arm imperiously and some eager minion came rushing forward with a suit ● I retired to a nearby station wagon, and after a breathless struggle with the change of attire in those confines I emerged—bent over, my crotch hauled up around my breastbone and my circulation already beginning to fail. With the hunched posture and halting gait of a penguin on his way to the drugstore for a laxative, I waddled over to Granatelli, feeling decidedly foolish. The suit was too small, and as I was wondering how the STP minion could have missed the correct size by such a wide margin, I noticed that Granatelli was vastly amused about something. The something, of course, was the suit, and it dawned on me that the choice of size was deliberate. Andy was gleeful at the successful joke he had played, and after this bit of hazing, I was genuinely famous and knows very well summoned to IRP to drive Granatelli's 4-wheel-drive Lotus wedge. The car was powered by a 318 cu. in. Plymouth V-8 with very exotic Weslake heads. Chrysler Corporation had invested heavily in this program and the program had not been, thus far, a success. In spite of the advantages of 4wd at Indy, the Plymouth-Lotus had not qualified. Later, at Continental Divide, the car ran slowly, and then abruptly left the road. Tests at IRP weren't helping. However attractive

Daytona 24 Hours, 1970
Ferrari 312 P

NART entered two Ferrari 312 Ps in the race. Tony Adamowicz and David Piper were driving one and Mike Parkes and I the other. I was coming down with mononucleosis, but I didn't know it until later.

Daytona was a demanding race. When you were on the banking, you had to crouch down to see ahead up the track, as if you were driving up a hill. The car was so low and the cockpit so cramped that I couldn't seem to crouch down enough. Carroll Smith was working as crew chief on the other car, but he also helped us. When I came in, he told me to get some sleep and put Parkes in for an extra stint. Then Parkes became exhausted and glanced the wall. Our fabricator, Wayne Sparling, hammered out the perfect replacement fender you can see here. Later, some rocks clogged our radiator. Between the two cars, we had one spare, and Carroll gave it to us. Adamowicz and Piper were ahead of us, but when their radiator suffered the same clog, they dropped out, giving us the class win and fourth overall.

NASCAR
Motor Trend 500, Riverside, 1970

This race at Riverside was the Motor Trend 500, the only road race of that NASCAR season. It drew a huge crowd, up there with all but the top oval events. Chrysler tried to improve their odds by hiring some road racers. Cotton Owens ran their second team. For the first team, they already had Dan Gurney, who'd won five of the last eight at Riverside. On the very slim chance of needing backup, they told Owens to hire me.

A week before the race, Chrysler arranged a test day at the track. Larry Rathgeb, an engineer from Chrysler, was there experimenting with an electronic timer and scorer that broke the lap into sections. The other drivers were Bobby Isaac, a top oval driver, and Dan Gurney. Once again, Pete Hutchinson had done me a tremendous favor. What a gift to be able to go out on the same track in the same equipment and compare yourself to the greatest.

The data came out printed on reels of paper. I laid them down on the floor of the motorhome — Dan's on top, mine and Bobby's below. The NASCAR guys never shifted, and Bobby was at a disadvantage at Riverside because he couldn't heel-toe on the downshifts. He didn't show much interest in the tests.

Turn five is a long, complex turn. The lines on the paper showed our speed at each point. I was nearly even with Dan going in; the big difference was coming out. He was giving up a little on the entry for a perfect exit. It was the old saw — exit speed was everything.

I qualified ninth, which Owens seemed to think was a good result. "If I'd known you was a real driver," he said, "I'd have given you a real car."

About a third of the way through the race, the engine blew up in spectacular fashion, as you can see. I spun the car, hoping to snuff out the flames. A week later, the car's regular driver, Buddy Baker, had the engine blow on him the same way. He said he remembered my move and replicated it, and it worked again.

A sidebar: a week or two after Riverside, the team invited me to Huntsville, Alabama for two days of testing a new automatic transmission that Rathgeb was developing. After the first day, a rep from Craftsman tools came up to me and offered me a ride in his sedan in a dirt-oval race that night. I qualified near the back. When the race began, I surged forward as the field in front of me seemed to bunch up. It wasn't until I was almost in the lead that I looked around and realized nobody else was racing; the yellow caution lights were still on. I dropped back into the last row. Still, my brief charge forward had been exhilarating. No one seemed too bent out of shape afterward, although the owner didn't offer me the car again for the next week.

Trans-Am, 1970
Dodge Challenger

When Pete Hutchinson was visiting our shop, Chrysler didn't yet have a team for the Trans-Am; Ray Caldwell and I asked what if we were that team? Then American Motors approached us with a deal to race for them. I went to test at Stardust, in Las Vegas, with John Cannon, Jerry Grant, and Skip Scott. I loved that track, and I was fastest in the test. We met the American Motors guys for breakfast at a fancy hotel in LA, expecting to sign the deal there, but the other guys were acting very strange. We found out that they had just signed with Roger Penske.

Hearts in our mouths, Ray and I called Pete Hutchinson to see whether a Dodge entry was still possible. Pete said he would be thrilled to have us.

We rented our shop from Reath Automotive for the year of the Trans-Am. It was in Long Beach in a line of commercial buildings all filled with automotive businesses. The big doors were open all the time, the temperature always a perfect 70.

One night, someone shouted for us to come to the door. Douglas had a factory across the freeway from us; they were moving the first DC-10 from one hanger to another. The plane could have been half a mile away, but it was so big as to be clearly visible at that distance, the moonlight shining on the silver body.

We stayed at a place called the Cloud Motel: "For the Rest of Your Life." Our body man, Ray Stonkus, broke his arm jumping into the hotel pool and had to work in a sling, gritting his teeth with every blow as he hammered out our fenders.

Ray Caldwell, the Dodge Challenger, and Sam Posey.
From: Autodynamics, 2 Bernard Street, Marblehead, Mass. 01945   (69-6648)

Men Of The Challenger
Talented Team For Dodge Effort

LONG BEACH, Calif., Mar. 17 — In just one month, the starter at the Laguna Seca race circuit in California will wave the green flag at a straining pack of brightly colored cars and the first Trans-American Sedan Championship race of 1970 will be under way.

As the cars storm up the hill, a green and black Dodge Challenger will be discernible near the front of the pack. At the wheel will be Sam Posey. Just a year before, Posey put a Formula A Eagle into victory lane at the end of Laguna's Continental Championship event.

Standing in the pits will be the captain of the Dodge TransAm team, Ray Caldwell. Surrounding him will be the group of specialists who built and prepared the racing Challenger. As it is this group who will be responsible for the success or failure of the Challenger effort, even more so than the young man

flying around the track, they deserve a close-up look.

As team manager, Caldwell's job is complex. While he is frequently slow to make an apparently easy decision, Caldwell is often trying to wrestle the problem into a place in his overall scheme of things. While some may find him frustrating to work with, he is unwaiveringly loyal to his crew. But no one will ever ground Ray Caldwell behind a desk; for him, total involvement is the way life is lived and . . . it is his formula for making cars win.

"THE GENERAL"

Caldwell's orders come from Peter Hutchinson. This young Chrysler executive, a 28-year-old maverick, has the job of coordinating Caldwell's Dodge and Dan Gurney's Plymouth activities. Hutchinson could probably do this job from his wood paneled office in Detroit. But, as an action man, known as "The General," he didn't like talking to his racing teams by long distance phone. He flew to Los Angeles and began using his penetrating and analytical mind to keep the operations of both Caldwell's and Gurney's teams under microscopic scrutiny. From his headquarters at a cluttered desk in Keith Black's engine building emporium he oversees the entire Chrysler TransAm effort and makes his most direct contribution to that effort: the development of the TransAm engines.

SAME BASIC ENGINE

Both teams will use basically the same engine configuration. It is a 340 Chrysler block destroked to 305cid. At this point the similarity between Posey's Challenger and Gurney's Barracuda ends. The Challenger wheelbase is two inches longer than the Barracuda's and Hutchinson and Caldwell have suspension for the Dodge. The car will have its own distinctive air

Chrysler's Dodge Division will be represented in the 1970 Trans-American Sedan Championship series by the Autodynamics-prepared Challenger. Though Chrysler's Pete Hutchinson coordinates the effort, principals in the future of Dodge's success are (l. to r.) chief mechanic Jack McCormack, driver Sam Posey and Autodynamics West's captain Ray Caldwell.

a surprise flight into the deep south to persuade two of Atlanta Firestone distributor Gene White's best men to join the team. He succeeded.

Thirty-year-old Ray Stonkus, one of the former White men, brings with him a wealth of practical experience gained in part in the preparation of NASCAR super rookie Pete Hamilton's Grand Touring Camaro. There just isn't another guy who has his knowledge in attacking his work with a rare ferocity Stonkus makes

mechanic on the Caldwell CanAm car. Whittier l. Autodynamics to form his o- company. Returning this spring help with the Challenger proje Whittier's prodigious strength be an undeniable asset during stops. Other part-time member the team will be Steve Green quick, young Chrysler man ferrets things that are tough to and John Whitman. Whitman timer in racing today.

MAKES DECISION

photographers, a PR man to direct the shoot, and even a model. Stuff like this — inane in every respect — can be curiously satisfying if you were a guy who'd just been racing in Formula 5000, which was definitely not The Big Time.

At some point, the car becomes more than a collection of pieces. Then the work is finished, and you're the first one to drive it. You pull out of pit lane, and it's a car. The first race was at Laguna Seca. Stonkus told me that if I came in with streaks of school-bus yellow from Parnelli's car down the side, he would buy me a drink; any other damage, I owed him the drink.

About five miles away, Dan Gurney had been in his shop at All American Racers, working on his Barracuda. I like to think our car grew on you, but his had

I had none of Mark's technical knowledge and could contribute nothing to the building of the car. Instead, Dodge took me to do some publicity shots. The cranks were in a corner of our shop. I don't have any idea what they were doing there. I felt like a complete idiot.

For another shot, they'd scouted this location in Hollywood — I'm not sure why. They sent a couple

a more conventional beauty — dark blue with large white numbers on the door. They got their parts from the factory before we did. They had Johnny Miller, AAR's top engine builder, and they had Dan.

The body for both cars was the same, the one that would go into the production Challengers and Barracudas. The first step was to dip it in a giant tub of acid that would wear

it away, for lightness. The key was how long to leave it in. In the opening tests, the Barracuda was faster, and we thought maybe we'd taken our car out of the acid too soon. But during tech, as the chief steward leaned on our roof, it caved in.

Pete Hutchinson called the nearest Dodge dealer and said we needed a car off the showroom floor. The dealer objected, but Hutchinson confirmed the order: The Big Time. We cut the roof off the car and welded it onto ours.

Now the roof was strong, but we had the same thin body. The first race was at Laguna Seca, which has that extremely sharp left/right combination coming down off the hill. About halfway through the race, I looked down at the transmission tunnel and could see about six inches of the road.

Moment of glory
Trans-Am, Elkhart Lake, 1970

Our engine builder was Keith Black, a guy who looked crusty but was very sophisticated in his thinking. Keith was the one who determined that Gurney was blowing us off with his engine. He bored out the cylinders again. When we arrived at Elkhart Lake, the effect was dramatic. We had the most power on the track where power is most important. You were allowed to cheat from time to time — you just couldn't overdo it.

In a high point of my year, I passed Parnelli Jones and Mark Donohue on the first lap to take the lead. It wasn't to last, and the photo shows why. My rear brakes were locking up — you can see the telltale skid marks.

This was to have been our best shot at a win all season, although at the time we thought we would have more. The car was at last finding its form. We still finished third despite the brakes.

Posey Third, Hall Fourth At Elkhart

(Continued from page 13)
Jones did the same with two more pit stops, leaving Savage with second place to himself and no hope of catching Donohue.

SWEDE BACKED OFF

"It wouldn't have been smart to try to catch Mark and I wanted to finish," commented Savage. "I backed off. All I could do was hope he'd break down."

That didn't happen though and it wasn't about to, with Donohue running at reduced speed and Penske giving him an occasional "EZ" sign to remind him everything was well under control.

SCCA TRANS-AMERICAN CHAMPIONSHIP RACE, ROAD AMERICA, ELKHART LAKE, WIS., JULY 19

FINISHERS: 1 - Mark Donohue, 1970 Javelin, 50 laps or 200 miles in 2.10:39.8 for an average speed of 91.839mph, $5200; 2 - Swede Savage, '70 Barracuda, 50 laps, $3700; 3 - Sam Posey, '70 Challenger, 50, $2550; 4 - Jim Hall, '70 Camaro, 50, $1800; 5 - Parnelli Jones, '70 Mustang, 50, $1600; 6 - Milt Minter, '69 Camaro, 50, $1400; 7 - Roy Woods, '69 Camaro, 49, $1200; 8 - Tony DeLorenzo, '70 Camaro, 49, $1000; 9 - Warren Agor, '70 Camaro, 48, $800; 10 - Gordon Dewar, '70 Camaro, 48, $700; 11 - Vince Gimondo, '69 Camaro, 47, $600; 12 - Warren Tope, '70 Mustang, 47, $500; 13 - Maurice Carter, '69 Camaro, 47, $400; 15 - Allen Hewitt, '67 Camaro, 45, $300; 16 - Larry Bock, '68 Camaro, 45, $250; 17 - Ed Hinchliff, '70 Mustang, 44, $200; 18 - Leigh Gardner, '67 Camaro, 44, $150; 19 - Dan Furey,

'69 Mustang, 43, $150; 20 - Bob Bienerth, '69 Camaro, 43, $100; 21 - Jerry Thompson, '70 Camaro, 43, $50; 22 - Jim Corwin, '68 Camaro, 38, $50; 23 - Dan Spiegel, '68 Chevy II, 37, $50; 24 - John Elliott, '69 Camaro, 37, $50; 25 - Levester Lewis, '69 Camaro, 31, $50.

DNF: 26 - Bob Fryer, '68 Camaro, 38, fire, $50; 27 - Ted Roberts, '69 Javelin, 26, engine failure, $50; 28 - Al LaBrush, '69 Camaro, 26, engine failure, $50; 29 - Ed Leslie, '70 Camaro, 25, engine failure; 30 - Peter Schwartzott, '70 Camaro, 22, engine failure; 31 - Gene Harrington, '70 Camaro, 17, engine failure; 32 - Bob McIntyre, '69 Camaro, 17, suspension failure; 33 - Peter Revson, '70 Javelin, 13, broken drive shaft; 34 - Duane Winkel, '69 Camaro, 2, lost wheel; 35 - George Follmer, '70 Mustang, 0, accident.

DISQ: J.A. Lagod, '68 Camaro, crew assistance in refueling on course.

With varied reactions, George Follmer, Parnelli Jones, Ted Roberts and Sam Posey (left to right) listen to instructions during the TransAm drivers' meeting. (Tony McCauley photo)

Sam Posey smokes his Dodge Challenger into a turn during action in the '70 series. Posey and the Ray Caldwell Autodynamics Challenger were consistently fast, but the first-year bugs and a few instances of over-enthusiastic driving kept the marque out of the winner's circle.
(Autoweek photo)

Posey was called into the pits for gas and fresh rubber on lap 65. His Autodynamics crew was quick, getting him out in 21 seconds.

Every week, the Dodge PR team prepared a press release: "Dodge wins..." They just had to fill in the name of the track. In fact, this was the only time we would lead all season.

But Jerry Titus's crash during the race overshadowed any results for the rest of us. Most of us were also in another form of racing conspicuously more dangerous. In this big block of a car, there didn't seem to be any way to hurt yourself. Jerry had a power-steering unit that none of us was using. It failed in the middle of a turn, and he couldn't react in time, crashing head-on into a stone abutment of a bridge that went over the track. We left him fighting for his life, and he died a few days later.

After Elkhart Lake, Keith felt that we had to go back to the regular engine. The handling was terrible, but Ray still wouldn't make any changes. He seemed to believe that the fault lay with the driver. Two races earlier, we'd been at Bridgehampton, a driver's track. By then, Dan had hired Swede Savage to drive one of the Barracudas. During practice, I asked Swede to take some laps in the Challenger. He came into the pits and said, "I couldn't make heads or tails of this car." It was a very gentlemanly thing to do. He was the young kid on the block; he could so easily have implied that I just wasn't giving the car a good ride.

During the race, the throttle was sticking. When I came in, Ray said he didn't think it was, implying that maybe I just had a light foot. I was so mad I jumped out of the car and stuck his head down in the carburetor to see for himself. It was pouring rain. Morale was at a low.

The next-to-last race was at Kent, Washington. By then, we'd hired Carroll Smith, who'd been the crew chief on the Ford that A.J. Foyt and Dan had driven to their classic win at Le Mans. He brought not only a vast amount of knowledge but an attitude that changed the team. We qualified well and finished third, ahead of Swede and everybody but Mark and Parnelli. It wasn't the win we needed to keep the program alive, but I felt we'd finally shown the potential I thought we had before the season.

Attacked by Revson
Trans-Am, Riverside, 1970

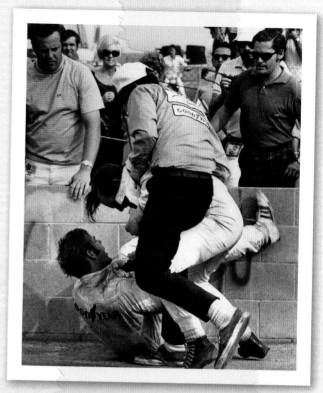

The last race of the season was at Riverside. Dodge hadn't renewed our contract, and it was to be the last race for our team. Right away, our brakes were locking up again. I felt the pressure to deliver a great drive at the last opportunity to change the minds at Dodge. I'd blown the start and was stuck behind Peter Revson. I thought I was faster, but he blocked me with relative ease.

The first turn following the start/finish is flat out in almost any car. Then comes a right-hander that you can take flat out with enough bravery and skill. I could do it maybe once a day. After a few laps, I got into Peter's draft approaching the right-hander. I pulled out to pass, my brakes locked up, and I hit him.

We both went off in the dust. I couldn't see anything. Somehow, we both wound up back on the track, with me ahead. Later that lap, I let him back by — something I'd never done before and wouldn't again.

I retired shortly after and was sitting on the pit wall watching Tony Adamowicz, in our other car. The next thing I knew, Peter had me by the throat and was throwing me down in pit lane. My team swarmed around us and yanked him off. Every photographer in the vicinity got the shots.

At the time, his reaction surprised me. The crash had almost no significance; we'd been fighting for seventh or eighth, the leaders nowhere in sight. A couple winters before, Peter and I had gone to Florida for a week of tarpon fishing with Jim Haynes and Harry Theodoracopulos,

cruising around in Harry's Maserati Quattroporte. I considered Peter a friend.

I like to think that we wound up on better terms. The next year, he helped me get my ride with Carroll Shelby at Lime Rock for $5,000. A few months later, at the 24 Hours of Daytona, I asked Luigi Chinetti whether I could choose my co-driver. I chose Peter, and Luigi paid him the most he paid anyone, around $5,000 — about a quarter of what some other owners were paying. We broke down.

Trying to outbrake Revson, Posey's rear brakes locked, causing him to make contact with Peter's car and both went off the track.

Le Mans, 1970
Ferrari 512 S

It rained for most of the race. My co-driver was Ronnie Bucknum, who did a beautiful job. I drove cautiously the whole way. The car had a tendency for the rear to jump out, and if it happened in the wet, you were lost. Luigi Chinetti was adamant about being careful. We finished fourth, the first Ferrari.

Ronnie Bucknum

My helmet
Buenos Aires 1000Km, 1971

I had always planned to design my helmet, and I thought my background in art would help. The stripes are there to suggest the American flag. In black and white photos, the red showed up as solid black and looked just as good.

The refined design of the helmet debuted in Argentina, at the 1971 Buenos Aires 1000Km, a prestigious sports-car race sanctioned by the FIA. I'd painted the helmet late the night before leaving, and it wouldn't dry, so I had the inspiration of putting it in the oven. That did the job. It turned the white to brown, and of course the fire burned out all the life-saving foam inside. I didn't have another helmet, so I wore it anyway.

We flew down in a cargo plane with our two cars. Five minutes after takeoff, we smelled gas. But one of our mechanics was on hand, found the gas had spilled from the tank of one of the cars, and cleaned it up.

No one seemed to look twice at my helmet that weekend except for Ignazio Giunti. At that time, he was Ferrari's new hot talent, racing every weekend somewhere around the world in the sports car they'd built for the FIA's 3-liter formula. He also turned out to share my interest in design. Just before the race, I saw him on the pit wall and introduced myself, and he remarked on my helmet. He didn't speak much English and I spoke no Italian, but we managed to strike up a brief conversation. He wanted to show me his helmet, but it was with his crew. I'd seen pictures of it before, and it was a beautiful thing — far more

Giunti's Ferrari

intricate than mine, a true work of art: the wings of a bird, remarkably detailed, on a green background with some cream pinstriping to set it off.

I never saw Giunti in the race — he was far ahead of me on the grid and pulled away. About a third of the way in, out of the last turn, I came on the remains of a fire. I saw enough of the car to know it was Giunti's. I was hoping he'd made it out all right. Minutes after the race, we learned that he'd died.

From Argentina, I flew to Milan to visit the Ferrari factory, on the same plane that was carrying Giunti's body. A large crowd had gathered at the airport to pay their respects. At the factory, it was a grim scene — rainy, cold, everyone thinking about Giunti. They had just finished work on the new car for Le Mans. Luigi Chinetti had sent me in his place to see it and thank everyone involved. They brought the car into a courtyard with a brick floor surrounded by some buildings. The car was pure red; it had no decals on it yet, not even the numbers or stripes. It was stunning. I hadn't prepared any Italian and didn't know what to say. Taking a chance, I said in English, "This car looks like a piece of shit." I'm not sure whether my attempt at levity went over or not.

My best Le Mans
Ferrari 512 M, 1971

The first photo on this page is tech inspection. It was downtown in Le Mans, at the plaza in front of the cathedral. At the end of the tech line, a guy waited with a small pot of black paint and a brush. He would put on your number by hand. He did it in a couple of minutes, perfectly every time.

Our pit was next to Penske's. Their car was a blue 512 M that they'd rebuilt in their shop in the US, and many felt it was the most beautiful Ferrari ever made. Penske was known for being better prepared and for managing all the details of a race better than anyone. The car looked like the proof of it. In many people's minds, Penske had already won the race.

In the first laps, my fuel pressure was fluctuating. I came into the pits, and they told me it was okay. Mr. Chinetti's usual instructions were to drive as slowly as possible. As I came blasting out of the pits, I recalled the advice; but after dropping so much time when the race had hardly begun, I felt justified in dismissing it, at least until I made up most of the distance to the leaders, as I knew the car could do. Mr. Chinetti could have signaled me to slow up, but reports say that he averted his eyes.

When I came in for my first scheduled stop, I heard a French pronunciation of my name and heard "lap record." Chinetti turned away, not wanting me to see he was pleased.

On their stop, Penske had replaced Mark Donohue with David Hobbs. He was right behind me as I came out of the pits.

In the right-hand S, it was a matter of pride to leave no more than six inches between the car and the guardrail, which was wattle, like bales of hay woven together. I noted with some satisfaction that I pulled out a little lead on David there each lap. Then a hundred yards farther on at Tertre Rouge, another tricky turn, he would pull back the gap.

Penske and NART had both wanted Ferrari's new engine. Before the race, they were debating in a garage just off the Mulsanne about who would get it. Mark disappeared, returned with a forklift, and drove off with the engine, settling the debate. In the race, it blew up after three hours, while ours lasted the whole way.

We finished third. The winners' circle then was a platform in the pits about five feet above the track, comprising plywood and 2x4s, with no railing. I was too tense to enjoy the moment; we'd had a problem with the

differential, and Tony Adamowicz drove around it brilliantly, but I was sure we'd violated an obscure rule of the race that no one else seemed to know — that you had to finish the last lap within a certain percent of your speed on your fastest lap. But I kept my mouth shut, and no one else ever mentioned the violation; I think the timers must just have overlooked it, with a capriciousness not unusual at Le Mans.

After one date in California, I had taken the chance of inviting Ellen to come with me to Le Mans, and she'd accepted. NART at Le Mans meant the Continental Hotel.

Mr. Chinetti had stayed there in his glory years in the 1950s. The shower was down a dark hall, and every room had a bidet. Ours overflowed every morning around dawn. Ellen and I put our suitcases on the bed.

The day after the race, we went back to the track just to soak up the scene. Luigi knew about a guy who made model cars. He had a stall in the midway. He'd carved a wooden model about three inches long of every Le Mans winner up until that year. The details were uncanny. I bought one of his three sets, for around $300.

The NART Ferrari 512M of Tony Adamowicz/Sam Posey sweeps past the GT-class-winning Porsche 911 of Touroul/Anselme. The Ferrari experienced a multitude of mechanical problems during the 24 hours and was 31 laps behind the winners at the flag—which was good enough for third overall.

Adamowicz/Posey Distant Third

The Ricordeau was a justifiably celebrated restaurant about half an hour from the track. We went there once a year. It was very small — ten tables, 40 people. After the race, we went there for lunch. Luigi Chinetti Jr. was our host. Between stints at the wheel, he'd managed to strike up a close friendship with the host's daughter. She served up the meal along with various innuendos.

The meal lasted at least three hours. I don't know how many courses appeared, but somehow we were never full. It was the quintessential French day, under the soft French skies. I had the girl of my dreams beside me. I was 27, and I'd just finished third in the world's greatest race. It was pure happiness.

Mount Equinox hill climb
Mercedes 300 SL, 1971

I'd been back from Le Mans for a couple weeks when our friend Jim Haynes suggested that we go to the Mount Equinox hill climb in Vermont. I drove up with my mom in the Mercedes 300 SL and we met Jim for dinner at the restaurant in the hotel at the top of the run. Over dinner, Jim said I should enter the 300 SL in the vintage class the next morning. I left our table, borrowed his Datsun 240Z, and made five runs up the course in the dark.

The climb was 5.2 miles long — in a curious coincidence, the same distance as a lap at Sebring at that time. Otherwise, the mountain hairpins didn't have much in common with Sebring's dead-flat runways. Close to the finish was a section they called the saddle, a ridge between two parts of the mountain that you could take at 120 mph if you had the guts; I didn't.

You raced the clock, going off one by one. My SL had an independent rear suspension that could be lethal in fast turns, as the outside tire tucked up under the chassis and wanted to steer the car off the road; Mercedes redesigned it in later models. But in a tight slow turn like the switchbacks of the climb, the flaw swung the car out into a perfect slide. All I had to do was turn in and wait for the right moment to put the throttle back on. I won the class with a record time. The trophy was four glasses hand-painted with pastoral scenes.

Boston Sunday Globe   July 4, 1971   A—15

CHANGE OF PACE—Sam Posey, international racing star, won vintage class in Mt. Equinox Hillclimb in this Mercedes 300 SL Gullwing. Just 5 minutes, 25 seconds after starter Don Brodie dropped the flag, Posey was at the top of the mountain for a new vintage class record. (Arthur Kelley photos)

Teaming up with Surtees
Questor Grand Prix, 1971

The morning after the last race of the Trans-Am season, John Whitman and Jack McCormack met with me for breakfast. I had been partners with Ray Caldwell since 1965. But over the breakfast, John, Jack, and I decided that I should go my own way.

I'm not sure how Ray felt about the decision; I know it was tough for me. But once I'd made it, I also felt relief. I knew that Jack would give the team some of his calm, easygoing character. We were starting fresh with a new sponsor. As we sat around the Denny's in Southern California with the light streaming in, the future looked promising.

After losing the Trans-Am deal with Dodge, Jack and I had decided to get back into Formula 5000. During the annual exposition of racing cars in England, we went over to see the new Lola, McLaren, and Surtees. The series had no works team until David Hobbs entered — you just bought a car, bolted a Chevy into it, and went racing.

Lola had a tube frame, and we liked the monocoques better. McLaren had a good car, but we thought we could be the top team for Surtees. We changed our return ticket so Jack could stay and work on the car. Surtees gave us space in his shop, which had a floor of hard-packed dirt.

One day, we went out to Goodwood for a test. The track was always misty and slick in the mornings. I was tense the whole way around. Jack took a lap to check the temperatures and pressures. When he came in, Denny Hulme stormed up to me. "Don't you ever let your mechanic in the car," he said. In fact, Jack had gotten one of his boots stuck among the pedals and was lucky to extricate it in time for the next corner.

Surtees and his chief mechanic were with us. We were eager for any help he would give us. Here he was, selling his first car to an American team — we thought he might have been anxious to sell more. But for ten days, he'd been the soul of British reserve. As we experimented with one setup after another, he didn't seem to be paying much attention. Then, in the last hour before we left, he poured out all the knowledge he had.

Our first race in the car was the Questor Grand Prix in California. It was for both Formula One and Formula 5000 cars. The works Ferrari team was there, and the Tyrrell team with Jackie Stewart driving. The prize money was huge. The race was by invitation only. We had our brand-new Surtees TS8 and a chance to make a mark around the top teams in Formula One. We were honored to be there.

Our Chevy engines were big, heavy, and had a lot of torque. The Formula One cars were faster at the top end. Only Mark Donohue was competitive with them. Early on, he was running as high as third or fourth before he broke down. Mario won. I made a mistake early, broke the nose, and went out — a dismal day.

More significant was that Swede Savage crashed during the race and hit his head. He'd been Dan Gurney's protégé, and afterward, Dan said he shouldn't be racing, but he didn't take Dan's advice. A year later, he was killed at Indy.

Mario's Ferrari Storms Ontario

Stewart 2nd At Questor GP

Sam Posey pitted at the same time to have a spoiler repaired. A shunt with John Cannon's STP March 701-Ford tore the nose section of Posey's ChampCarr Surtees TS8-Chevy. The nose section was replaced but overheating caused a blown head gasket which put Posey out

QUESTOR GRAND PRIX GRID

No. 8-Jackie Stewart Tyrrell-Ford 1:41.227, 113.620mph (G)	No. 10-Chris Amon Matra-Simca MS120 1:41.275, 113.536mph (G)
4-Jacky Ickx Ferrari 312B 1:41.531, 113.250 (F)	6-Denis Hulme McLaren M19-Ford 1:42.458, 112.225 (G)
12-Pedro Rodriguez BRM 160 1:42.473, 112.209 (F)	19-Graham Hill Brabham BT34-Ford 1:42.763, 111.892 (G)
26-Mark Donohue Lola T192-Chevrolet 1:43.211, 111.406 (G)	14-Jo Siffert BRM 153 1:43.350, 111.256 (F)
2-Emerson Fittipaldi Lotus 72-Ford 1:43.358, 111.248 (F)	27-George Follmer Lotus 71-Ford 1:43.474, 111.123 (F)
3-Reine Wisell Lotus 72-Ford 1:43.535, 111.058 (F)	5-Mario Andretti Ferrari 312B 1:43.542, 111.050 (F)
18-Henri Pescarolo March 701-Ford 1:43.709, 110.871 (G)	20-Tim Schenken Brabham BT33-Ford 1:43.772, 110.804 (G)
30-Sam Posey Surtees TS8-Chevrolet 1:44.128, 110.425 (F)	15-Howden Ganley BRM 153 1:44.739, 109.781 (F)
21-Ronnie Peterson March 711-Ford 1:44.360, 110.180 (F)	7-Peter Gethin McLaren M14A-Ford 1:45.310, 109.186 (G)
17-Derek Bell March 711-Ford 1:44.977, 109.532 (G)	29-Ron Grable Lola T190-Chevrolet 1:45.402, 109.090 (G)
37-Lou Sell Lola T192-Chevrolet 1:45.397, 109.096 (G)	31-Peter Revson Surtees TS8-Chevrolet 1:45.668, 108.816 (G)
35-Bob Bondurant Lola T192-Chevrolet 1:45.528, 108.960 (G)	33-Al Unser Lola T192-Chevrolet 1:48.172, 106.297 (F)
4-Tony Adamowicz Lola T192-Chevrolet 1:47.831, 106.633 (G)	36-Gus Hutchison ASD American-Chevrolet 1:50.954, 103.632 (G)
38-Bobby Unser Lola T192-Chevrolet 1:48.512, 105.964 (G)	28-A.J. Foyt McLaren M10B-Chevrolet 1:52.229, 102.454 (G)
32-Swede Savage Eagle-Plymouth 1:51.509, 103.116 (G)	
F - Firestone	G - Goodyear

With Swede Savage

Mark Donohue's Lola (26) and Mario Andretti's Ferrari overtake Sam Posey's Surtees exiting turn nine on the Ontario Motor Speedway road course. Donohue, strongest of the Formula A entries, ran as high as third in the first heat before experiencing oiling difficulties. Andretti went on to win both heats.

(Pete Biro photo)

Rivalry with Hobbo
Formula 5000, 1971

In 1971, Formula 5000 reached its maturity. We had the cars and the drivers, and I like to think the duels between David Hobbs and me gave the season a focal point.

After four or five races, a pattern emerged. I would get the pole, and David would win the race. The Surtees was a wonderful car for qualifying; you could find the limit right away. But in the first five laps of the race, David would drive away from me. We had Goodyear tires and he had Firestones. I now think that his tires might have heated up faster. It would have taken Mark Donohue 30 seconds to pick out what was wrong.

I knew I could trust David's driving in close quarters, and I hope he felt the same about me. We would exchange the lead two or three times in a race, but we never hit each other or ran each other off the road. In these shots, David is in car #10.

With Jack McCormack

Laguna Seca: Hobbs (10) to my left, Bucknum (51) and Matich (3) following

'Motor Mouth' Gets Cranked On To Snatch Mid-Ohio Pole

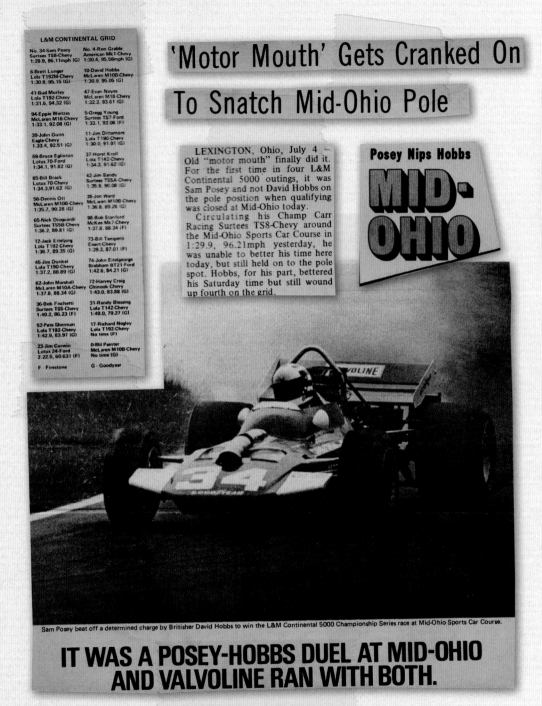

Sam Posey beat off a determined charge by Britisher David Hobbs to win the L&M Continental 5000 Championship Series race at Mid-Ohio Sports Car Course.

IT WAS A POSEY-HOBBS DUEL AT MID-OHIO AND VALVOLINE RAN WITH BOTH.

The cigarette company L&M was sponsoring the series. One of their PR men would go to each race to arrange interviews the Friday before. Soon David and I began trading barbs. People seemed to find it amusing, and we went with it. David was winning all the races, but he would play up the rivalry: Sam, you better watch out this weekend... I now think those interviews helped both of us move into careers in television. The irony was that they were also the start of one of my closest friendships. My wife, Ellen, did the "Peace on Earth" drawing.

David ran away with the season, but I had one highlight. Bill Edgar, the owner of a small film company, somehow sold a special on David and me to Pepsi. He brought his crew to Mid-Ohio. It was a two-heater; David beat me in the first by a car length, and I won the second by a little more, giving me the overall win. If the movie was all you'd seen of the championship, you might have thought I'd won it.

Front-row qualifiers Ron Grable (left) in the Williams Racing American Mk1-Chevy and Sam Posey in the ChampCarr Surtees TS8-Chevy lead David Hobbs' Hogan McLaren M10B-Chevy (10) and the tightly-bunched Mid-Ohio Continental 5000 Championship field toward the green flag for the fourth round of the L&M series. (Bill Fox photo)

DAVID HOBBS HAS HADDIT

UP TO HERE!

That's David on the left. He had just finished about this far behind Sam Posey in the 1971 Mid-Ohio L&M Championship and wasn't too impressed with Sam "The Mouth That Roared" Posey getting the flagon of grape and some fat smacks from Miss Mid-Ohio.

Frank Matich climaxed victory circle festivities by firmly applying racing tape to the otherwise unstoppable mouth of "Silent Sam" Posey. The verbal sparring between Posey, Matich and David Hobbs was only slightly overshadowed by racing. (Autoweek photos)

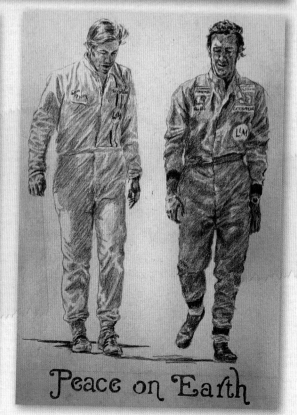

Peace on Earth

Formula One
Watkins Glen, 1971 and 1972

A ride in Formula One is the best one a driver can aspire to. In those days, it was common for a team to enter a third car, for a driver from the home country of the race. After the end of the Formula 5000 season, Jack McCormack pressed John Surtees to give me a ride in the United States Grand Prix at Watkins Glen.

Surtees agreed. But when Jack and I arrived at the track a day early, we learned that the team's sponsor had nominated Gijs van Lennep to replace Rolf Stommelen in the third car. Van Lennep had won Le Mans that year and was a hot property. He was on a plane to Watkins Glen. Surtees told me that the fairest decision he could think

L-R Ronnie Petersen, Carlos Reutemann, Andrea deAdamich, Carlos Pace, Reine Wisell, Wilson Fittipaldi, Niki Lauda, Henri Pescarolo, Jody Schecter. Brian Redman, Emerson Fittipaldi, Sam Posey, Derek Bell, Tim Schenken, Jacky Ickx, Dave Walker, Mario Andretti, J.P. Beltoise, Howden Ganley, Chris Amon, Peter Revson, Clay Regazzoni, Francois Cevert, Patrick Depallier, Mike Beutler.

Surtees TS9 US GP 1971

of was to give each of us a few laps and see who was fastest.

I went out first and did five laps that would have put me about midfield at the start. Gijs was slower. I went out again. I didn't want to record any slow laps, so when I felt a little off, I pitted, leaving a series of improving times. Van Lennep didn't improve in his second stint. Whether he was jet-lagged or not, I didn't care; the ride was mine. In every sense, as corny as it sounds, it was a dream come true.

I qualified in midfield. With the other engines all around me, I couldn't hear mine, and I blew the standing start. The rest of the race was an anticlimax. But I felt at the time that I wouldn't forget it, and I haven't.

The next year, Jack made the same deal with Surtees. I didn't qualify any better than the year before, but this time I finished the race, in 12th place — the best of the drivers without a regular ride.

Tim Schenken chases

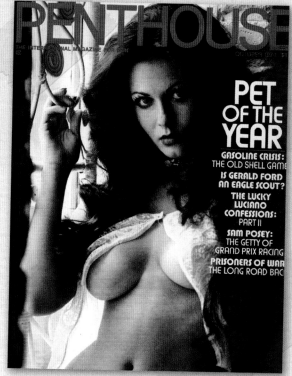

PENTHOUSE

THE INTERNATIONAL MAGAZINE FOR MEN

PET OF THE YEAR

GASOLINE CRISIS:
THE OLD SHELL GAME

IS GERALD FORD
AN EAGLE SCOUT?

THE LUCKY
LUCIANO
CONFESSIONS:
PART II

SAM POSEY:
THE GETTY OF
GRAND PRIX RACING

PRISONERS OF WAR
THE LONG ROAD BACK

INDEPENDENTS

SAM POSEY

Sam Posey, the highest placed rookie finisher at Indianapolis and Pocono this year (fifth at each race), is driving his own Surtees F1 car here this weekend. Third place holder in the season point standings in the L&M 5000 series, Sam also has competed in nearly every type of road racing machine — from factory prototypes in enduros to boxy Trans-Am sedans. This is his third weekend of competition this year at The Glen — he competed in both the June L&M weekend and the July Six-Hours event.

USGP '72

STARTING GRID

Hulme McLaren-Ford 1'41"08	Revson McLaren-Ford 1'40"53	Stewart Tyrrell-Ford 1'40"48
Reutemann Brabham-Ford 1'41"69		Cevert Tyrrell-Ford 1'41"45
Scheckter McLaren-Ford 1'42"06	Amon Matra-Simca 1'41"98	Regazzoni Ferrari 1'41"95
	Andretti Ferrari 1'42"48	E. Fittipaldi JPS-Ford 1'42"40
W. Fittipaldi Brabham-Ford 1'42"77	Ickx Ferrari 1'42"80	Depailler Tyrrell-Ford 1'42"52
	Pace March-Ford 1'43"32	Hailwood Surtees-Ford 1'43"20
Beltoise BRM 1'44"24	Ganley BRM 1'44"08	Wisell JPS-Ford 1'43"54
	Barber March-Ford 1'44"28	de Adamich Surtees-Ford 1'44"28
Posey Surtees-Ford 1'44"53	Pescarolo March-Ford 1'44"43	Beuttler March-Ford 1'44"37
	Lauda March-Ford 1'45"28	Redman BRM 1'44"93
Gethin BRM 1'46"60	Hill Brabham-Ford 1'46"31	Peterson March-Ford 1'46"14
	Walker JPS-Ford 1'50"60	Bell Tecno-Ford 1'47"02
		Schenken Surtees-Ford 1'57"67

RESULTS

	Drivers	Make	Laps	Time
1	STEWART	Tyrrell-Ford	59	1.41'45"35
2	CEVERT	Tyrrell-Ford	59	+ 37"43
3	HULME	McLaren-Ford	59	+ 42"73
4	PETERSON	March-Ford	59	+ 1'22"52
5	ICKX	Ferrari	59	+ 1 23'12
6	ANDRETTI	Ferrari	58	
7	DEPAILLER	Tyrrell-Ford	58	
8	REGAZZONI	Ferrari	58	
9	SCHECKTER	McLaren-Ford	58	
10	WISELL	JPS-Ford	57	
11	HILL	Brabham-Ford	57	
12	POSEY	Surtees-Ford	57	
13	BEUTTLER	March-Ford	57	
14	PESCAROLO	March-Ford	57	
15	AMON	Matra-Simca	57	
16	BARBER	March-Ford	57	
17*	HAILWOOD	Surtees-Ford	56	
18*	REVSON	McLaren-Ford	54	
+	LAUDA	March-Ford	49	

* = DNF but classified

+ = not classified (less than 90 % of the total distance)

RETIREMENTS

Drivers	Make	Laps	
Bell	Tecno	8	overheating
E. Fittipaldi	JPS-Ford	17	roadholding troubles
Schenken	Surtees-Ford	22	suspension
de Adamich	Surtees-Ford	25	accident
Reutemann	Brabham-Ford	31	engine
Redman	BRM	34	engine
Beltoise	BRM	40	engine
W. Fittipaldi	Brabham-Ford	43	engine
Ganley	BRM	44	engine
Walker	JPS-Ford	44	engine
Gethin	BRM	47	engine
Pace	March-Ford	48	engine
Revson *	McLaren-Ford	54	ignition
Hailwood *	Surtees-Ford	56	accident

* = classified

Afterward, Surtees talked to me about driving in Europe in Formula Two and occasionally Formula One. Formula Two at that time was hellaciously dangerous, and I declined what turned out to be my best chance at the highest form of racing. But I still have a few treasured souvenirs of a brief Formula One career, including the photo of the drivers' meeting (heady company), and the lap chart, program, and *Penthouse*. Someone even made a beautiful model of my 1971 car.

Can-Am finale
McLaren M8E, Riverside, 1971

R oy Woods hired me for an end-of-season drive at
Riverside. I finished fourth, which was as high as I ever
achieved in the Can-Am, and I can't remember a thing about
it, except that the car was very beautiful in pictures.

Racing | Sam Posey

Indy
Eagle-Offy, 1972

Over the previous year, Jack McCormack had made a point of going up to Dan Gurney's All American Racers and keeping in touch with the guys there. Johnny Miller was their engine builder, and Jack became good friends with him. Johnny whispered in Jack's ear to have a look at their latest project. Jack put a down payment on the first customer chassis then and there.

By the time we had to buy the car, we still didn't have a sponsor. By then, Bobby Unser had set record laps at Ontario in the prototype. At least 20 other customers were in line. Dan told us he would lend us his ace PR man, Max Mullman, for one week, to help us find the money. If we couldn't, he would have to take us off the list.

Ken Norris ran a metal-stamping business that was the first to create a seamless bullet cartridge. Their other products ranged from toilet seats to giant tanks for containing contents under pressure. Ken reasoned that sponsoring a racing team might bring some unity to the disparate branches of his company. Mullman made the deal. Ken couldn't have been a more agreeable sponsor.

I did the paint job for the car, and I believe it was the most beautiful in the race, with the possible exception of Mark Donohue's dark-blue Penske. AAR could only build three or four chassis before Indy. We were one of the lucky few to have one. It was clear from the first laps early in May that it was the car to have.

Herb Porter had built the engines for all the Goodyear

teams who wanted them. He stood on the grid during qualifying. As you came up, he would take out a wrench and set the boost pressure for the run, based on his hunch and the weather and what others were doing. He inspired reverence and a little fear. When he saw me, he took a quarter turn with his wrench, looked at me again, and took another quarter turn — maybe thinking I was going to need some help from the engine. I believe only Bobby Unser had more power than I did.

As you wait to go out, you don't look at the crowd, but you know it's there — 200,000 people watching. You're in a line, and then the track is empty in front of you. Harlan Fengler, the chief steward, waved us out. He wore a hat with a bird feather sticking out the top.

The first lap is a warm-up. You had to let the Offy get up to temperature by driving a whole lap at 20 mph, also zigzagging to warm up the tires. On the second lap, you punched the throttle coming out of turn two. After all the waiting, I was just happy the moment had come.

We'd been there three weeks without making a run at top speed. With the boost tweaked, the acceleration down the back straight was the most I would feel all season. By turn three, you're at qualifying speed.

On the front straight, you see the green flag. You have four more laps, the green waving each time you pass the start/finish. Your average speed over the four flying laps determines your qualifying. Your pit crew stands at the wall and signals you with the speed for each lap as you're coming around at the end of the next. They have to decide before

the checker — before they know your speed for the last lap — whether to accept the run or call it off. You get three total chances to qualify. It was a tense decision for Jack.

Bobby Unser had the pole. I knew his time was out of reach. The difference between second and fifth didn't seem as important as making sure we got in the race. I made a deliberate attempt not to let the event carry me away. Still, I didn't feel I'd left much on the table.

As you come into the pits, the crew surrounds the car. Jack had my speed. I was third or fourth. That's when you start breathing deeply and praying that the other guys still to come make a mistake.

After your run, you drive up in pit lane to a spot where they take your photo with the car. Next you get a shot together with the crew. It was a tradition at Indy that the

SAM POSEY & CREW
INDIANAPOLIS MOTOR SPEEDWAY – 1972

MONDAY, MAY 15, 1972

Qualifying Table

FIRST ROW

BOBBY UNSER		GARY BETTENHAUSEN		MARIO ANDRETTI	
No. 6 Olsonite		No. 7 Sunoco		No. 9 Viceroy	
EAGLE TURBO-OFFY—G		McLAREN TURBO-OFFY—G		PARNELLI TURBO-OFFY—F	
TIME	SPEED	TIME	SPEED	TIME	SPEED
:46.17	194.932	:47.50	189.474	:47.68	188.758
:46.91	196.036	:47.60	189.076	:47.84	188.127
:45.91	196.036	:47.68	188.758	48.17	186.838
:45.89	196.121	:47.82	188.206	48.19	186.761
TOTALS		TOTALS		TOTALS	
3:03.73	195.940	3:10.60	188.877	3:11.88	187.617

SECOND ROW

JOE LEONARD		SAM POSEY		JOHN RUTHERFORD	
No. 1 Samsonite		No. 34 Norris		No. 18 Patrick	
PARNELLI TURBO-OFFY—F		EAGLE TURBO-OFFY—G		BRABHAM TURBO-OFFY—G	
TIME	SPEED	TIME	SPEED	TIME	SPEED
:48.71	184.767	:48.76	184.578	:49.06	183.449
:48.40	185.950	:48.64	185.033	:49.08	183.374
:48.43	185.835	:48.79	184.464	:49.23	182.815
:48.82	184.351	:49.06	183.449	:49.10	183.299
TOTALS		TOTALS		TOTALS	
3:14.36	185.223	3:15.25	184.379	3:16.47	183.234

THIRD ROW

ART POLLARD		LLOYD RUBY		SWEDE SAVAGE	
No. 40 STP Oil Treatment		No. 5 Wynn's		No. 42 Michner Industries	
LOLA TURBO-FORD—F		ATLANTA TURBO-FORD—F		EAGLE TURBO-OFFY—G	
TIME	SPEED	TIME	SPEED	TIME	SPEED
:49.85	180.542	:49.80	180.723	:49.52	181.745
:49.26	182.704	:49.56	181.561	:49.41	182.149
:49.19	182.964	:49.55	181.635	:49.50	181.818
:49.91	180.325	:49.52	181.745	:49.67	181.196
TOTALS		TOTALS		TOTALS	
3:18.21	181.626	3:18.44	181.415		

FOURTH ROW

JIM HURTUBISE		JOHN MARTIN	
No. 56 Miller High Life		No. 89 Unsponsored	
COYOTE TURBO-FORD—F		BRABHAM TURBO-OFFY—F	
TIME	SPEED	TIME	SPEED
:49.82	180.650	:50.14	179.497
:49.57	181.561	:50.06	179.784
:49.75	180.905	:50.16	179.426
:49.70	181.087	:50.07	179.748
TOTALS		TOTALS	
3:18.84	181.050	3:20.43	179.614

80,000 See Race Lineup

Take Shape

INDIANAPOLIS MOTOR SPEEDWAY CORPORATION

NOT GOOD FOR GATE ADMISSION — Good on Race Day Only When Used With Official Badge — MAY 27TH 1972

56th INTERNATIONAL 500-MILE SWEEPSTAKES

9

FORM 380-5083
Dennison Eastman Corp. L.A.
FLT. 09-93-05
STAND BY

GARAGE AREA
1972 GASOLINE ALLEY INDIANAPOLIS 500
307
Not Good for Gate Admission April 29, 1972—May 21, 1972
VISITING HOURS 9:00 A.M.—6:00 P.M.
Not Good on Race Day
DATE — Tony Hulman

THE NEWS
Blue Streak
INDIANAPOLIS, INDIANA, SATURDAY, MAY 20, 1972
103rd YEAR — 10 CENTS

car owner didn't wear the team uniform. Here you can see Fred Carillo in a Hawaiian shirt. When they took the photo, I didn't yet know where we'd qualified, but I thought we were in the race. In the end, I was seventh.

I'd qualified on the first weekend, so we had the next weekend off. I went out to Seattle for a Formula 5000 race. There I made the grave PR mistake of telling a reporter that Indy was Indy, of course, but my heart was in Formula 5000 and road racing. I thought I was playing

Fast Sam Does A Lot Of Talking

Sam Posey spent a good deal of time on the telephone yesterday — receiving some "well dones" from friends, spreading some of his exhuberence to his mother and girl friend and just doing what he likes—talking.

Posey had good reason to be rosey because he had just completed phase one of his Indianapolis Motor Speedway goals.

POSEY qualified for his first 500 yesterday at 184.379. It put him in the middle of the second row for the immediate future and also made him the fastest rookie for the time being.

Since there are still five drivers who were in the original "pole line" on Saturday, Posey's final position won't be established until next weekend.

But one thing was established—Posey showed a lot of people he was a pretty darned good racer after all.

"At this point I must say I do feel rather happy about the whole thing," said the loquacious 28-year-old from Capistrano, Calif.

"I'm a little tired but I feel much better than I did Saturday."

On the opening day of time trials, Sam spun his new Norris Eagle in the first turn. But yesterday was a new story and Sam continues the telling.

"I really couldn't let down completely or couldn't keep built up to qualify because of the constant on and off of the rain.

"I've got a good machine, a good crew and we're in pretty good shape," said the man who got his start in sports cars.

POSEY hasn't had as much success at Indy as he has in his various road course ventures.

In 1969 he came to Indianapolis and was requested to get more experience. In '70 he spun out while trying to qualify and last May he was bumped from the field.

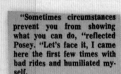

"Sometimes circumstances prevent you from showing what you can do," reflected Posey. "Let's face it, I came here the first few times with bad rides and humiliated myself.

"They talk about drivers' ability and all that but when it comes right down to it there isn't that much difference between us. It's the equipment.

"And don't get me wrong, drivers do make mistakes or turn in awfully brilliant performances like Bobby did. I never considered myself a rookie when I came here because I'd been a professional driver for five years.

"Now I hope some people will realize that I am becoming more accomplished."

Sam is the first one to admit that he still has plenty to learn.

"I don't think I'll win this race this year," predicts the friendly young man, "but some day . . ."

And it will be a great interview when he does. ROBIN MILLER

it cool — avoiding some false pandering — but the take was Posey shuns Indy. Every newspaper in Indiana picked it up.

The night before the race, John Whitman, Jack, and Ellen and I went to dinner at the restaurant on the top floor of the airport hotel. For those few days, people knew you around the track, and we wanted a quiet place. During the dinner, the four of us talked over what I should do. It was my first Indy, the race could be overwhelming, and I didn't want to make a rookie mistake. But John countered that this might also be my only chance. I heard everyone out, not sure what to think.

The next morning, Ellen and I were up at about five, sitting cross-legged on our bed at the Howard Johnson's. Ellen's presence kept me calm. Each driver at the hotel had a policeman on a Harley ready to escort us to the track. We went straight to the garage, and I did a few interviews that we'd agreed to beforehand, which also had a calming effect. Then Jack took the car out to the grid. As he opened the door to the garage, the crowd sounded like a waterfall close by.

I couldn't resist stepping outside the garage for the anthem and Back Home Again in Indiana. But I wanted to avoid the grid. I didn't go out for almost an hour. By then, the start wasn't far away.

I don't remember much from the

parade laps. At the start, they were using a new signaling system that not everyone understood. Half the field was lagging back. I was at full speed, coming up on the leaders, at the line. On the back straight, I nestled in behind Mario. The heat from his turbo was an uncanny green. I drafted him in the turn and passed him coming out of turn four.

In my rear view, I could see him struggling with the car. It crossed my mind that I could never drive like that. I just knew I was out of my league. Bobby Unser was streaking away into the distance. At the end of the second lap, I backed off. Mario and three or four other guys passed me.

After 15 or 20 minutes, the engine misfired down the back straight. I coasted through the last two turns and into the pits. Jack looked in the car, smiled at me without saying anything, and flipped a lever under my knees to allow the fuel to pass from the tank on the left side of the car to the one on the right. I was supposed to have moved the lever myself after 20 laps, but it had just escaped me. The pipe was a few inches in diameter. Back on the track, I could feel the cold under my legs as the fuel shifted from the inside to the outside tank. The mistake was the end of my chances to win, but it might have been a blessing. It took any pressure off me to push too hard.

Tony Bettenhausen, whose bad luck at Indy was infamous, was driving for Penske that year, in the second car behind Mark. He was leading at half distance, on his way to the win. He broke down on the back straight. I saw his car off in the grass, gleaming in the sun, and felt a moment of sympathy for him.

A little later, Lloyd Ruby lapped me, giving me a wave as he went by. I had a habit of checking my inside mirror every time I went into turn one or three. The next time I checked it, all that remained was the steel stalk. Something had flown off Ruby's car and cut it off, about six inches from my helmet.

Before the race, Peter Revson had told me that many of the Indy veterans came from sprint cars and weren't fit enough to go the full 500 miles at top speed. In the month before the race, I'd spent a few minutes in my hotel room each night holding a chair out in front of me and twisting my arms back and forth as if turning a wheel. Inspired by Tom Wolfe's *The Right Stuff*, I also tried some long division while sitting in a sauna. Peter was right: I passed five or six cars in the last hundred miles and was closing on Sammy Sessions in fifth at the finish.

I don't remember the checkered flag, dinner that night, or the banquet the next — only sitting in the car in the sunny pits after the finish. Jim McKay and Chris Economaki came to congratulate me. Jim said, "That makes you rookie of the year." I was sure it did. The award ended up going to Mike Hiss.

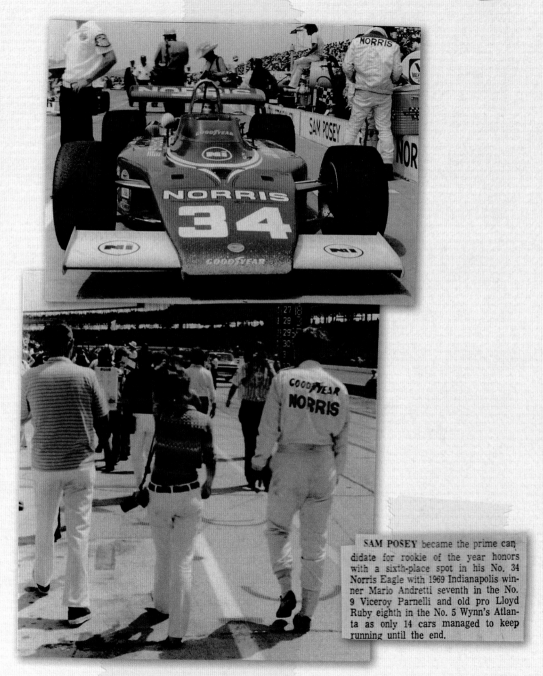

SAM POSEY became the prime candidate for rookie of the year honors with a sixth-place spot in his No. 34 Norris Eagle with 1969 Indianapolis winner Mario Andretti seventh in the No. 9 Viceroy Parnelli and old pro Lloyd Ruby eighth in the No. 5 Wynn's Atlanta as only 14 cars managed to keep running until the end.

500 Top 10

1—MARK DONOHUE

2—JERRY GRANT

3—AL UNSER

4—JOE LEONARD

5—SAM SESSIONS

6—SAM POSEY

THE INDIANAPOLIS STAR

"Where the spirit of the Lord is, there is Liberty"—II Cor. 3-17

Mark Donohue Wins Indy 500

Jerry Grant 2nd, Then 12th

By Ray Marquette
USAC Editor

INDIANAPOLIS — Mark Donohue had his day in the sun and Victory Lane—May 27th by winning the biggest plum of his racing career.

The man from Newtown Square, Pa., led for only 13 laps of the 56th Indianapolis 500-mile race but they were the big ones that took him right to the bank as he scored his first Indy triumph with a record speed average of 162.962mph in the No. 66 Sunoco McLaren.

It didn't matter a bit to Donohue that he led only the final 13 circuits around the famous 2.5-mile race track because he was the first car to take the checkered flag and is expected to collect more than $200,000 of the $1 million purse to be split up at the Victory Banquet Monday night.

It did matter a lot to Jerry Grant, second-place finisher in the No. 48 Mystery Eagle of Dan Gurney. It mattered so much that Gurney took a look at the official results when they were posted then filed a $100 protest fee so he could check the scoring tapes and see if Grant, not Donohue, might be the winner.

"It was a great race and a great finish no matter who won," said Gurney.

The crowd of 275,000-plus had to agree as an unscheduled pit stop by Grant on the 186th lap to change a badly-damaged left front tire took an apparent victory right out of his grasp and handed it to Donohue—at least for the moment.

Gurney withdrew his protest

(Continued on page 26)

Count Ghislain de Vogue

Maison Moet et Chandon

and

Mr. Anton Hulman Jr.

Indianapolis Motor Speedway

cordially invite you to a

Champagne Party

immediately following

The Indianapolis 500

Golfers' Lounge
Speedway Motel

May 27, 1972

That night, I would move up to fifth when Jerry Grant, in second, was penalized for a fueling infraction. Mark had won. Could I ever escape him and his infernal luck — or superiority? But something about it also felt right: He won, I was fifth — business as usual.

The keys above are from our room at the Speedway Motel. If you had a room one year, they reserved it for you the next — unless you turned it down. I still had my reservation when I covered the race for TV years later.

Bulletproof Ferrari
Le Mans 24 Hours, 1972

In 1972, the organizers at Le Mans were afraid of how fast the top cars had become, and they changed the rules. In place of the long-tail Ferrari, Mr. Chinetti entered a coupe, the Ferrari Daytona. Believing the Daytona to be bulletproof, he told us to race all out — there was no other way to win — proving that his earlier advice was based on the situation, not some cautious temperament. A man named Pozzi had fielded an identical car, almost down to the paint job, and they were also going all out. For more than half the race, we duked it out, our names indistinguishable in the PA's narration of the battle. Pozzi won it, finishing first in class and fifth overall; we were sixth.

Mom's Citroën
The evocative 'Traction Avant'

Bernard Cahier was a first-class photographer and a man of the world. I knew him because he was also the Goodyear representative at Le Mans. The Goodyear tent always had a warm feeling; the booze flowed freely, the celebrities gathered there, and the rest of us all followed. Once a year, I would see Bernard for a fair stretch at Le Mans, where he would also take pictures throughout the race, out covering it in the rain, through the night.

With Bernard, the conversation was never limited to racing. I told him that my mom had a particular love for the pre-war front-drive Citroën. It looked a little like the kind of car gangsters drove here in the 30s. Bernard said, "Well, I can get you one." He knew the head of a department at Citroën that was like a forerunner of today's pre-owned used dealers — they restored the cars for celebrities at no charge. Somehow he thought we could fit in this category.

I never expected anything to come of the conversation. Then, maybe six months later, I received a call from Luigi Chinetti, also a friend of Cahier's, who said our car was here, at a dock in Newark. Luigi brought it to his Ferrari dealership in Greenwich, and I arrived late in the evening. There was the car, immaculate, the keys in the ignition. I started home at about 2 a.m. with no license plate or registration. In those days they had a pay phone in the shopping center in town. I called my mom and told her to meet me outside the house. She was waiting in her nightgown as I pulled up. I said, "Let's go for a ride." The last thing my father-in-law saw

With Mom

LA 7 CITROËN

PRIX: 17.700 FRS.

DE CONCEPTION ENTIÈREMENT NOUVELLE

MANIABILITÉ, TENUE DE ROUTE ET ADHÉRENCE INÉGALABLES
TRACTION AVANT - " MOTEUR FLOTTANT " A CULBUTEURS
ROUES INDÉPENDANTES - FREINS HYDRAULIQUES
SUSPENSION PAR BARRES DE TORSION
CARROSSERIE " TOUT-ACIER " MONOCOQUE
VOITURE INTÉGRALEMENT AÉRODYNAMIQUE
VITESSE : 100 KM. POIDS : 900 KG. CONSOMMATION : 9 L. AUX 100 KM.

LIVRAISON IMMÉDIATE

was his wife heading down her driveway into the dark with a strange man in a strange car.

The car became a valuable possession in our family — a sort of symbol of the possibility for a fairytale to come true — and we never sold it. But at some time, it stopped running. My friend Don Breslauer, a virtuoso mechanic who lives not far from us, determined that to fix the car would involve removing the whole front end. We decided that if he could fix it, he could have it. Working on his own dime, he restored it to its full potential. Now he often does me the favor of driving it over to our house for a visit.

Don Breslauer

A season to forget
Formula 5000, 1972

For the 1972 Formula 5000 season, I had another Surtees, the TS11. Here I am on the front row for the second race, at Edmonton, with my friend and former teammate Brett Lunger on the pole: a promising start, but my engine blew in the first heat.

David Hobbs was back with a Lola. The car looked spectacular with its huge radiators at the back and long sloping nose. But it just wasn't a good car — both slow and unreliable. My main adversary was Graham McRae.

McRae was enterprising and fearless. When it rained at Mosport, he thought he needed a deeper tread on his tires, so he just got out a spoon and carved into them. He kept to himself, showing no interest in making friends around the paddock.

McRae would qualify eighth or ninth and be second after a few laps. He would come flying off the slow turns. Cheating was a given in the Tasman series, where he'd been driving. I pressed the officials to weigh his car, but they never would.

In these photos of McRae and me, I'm receiving his consolation prize — Woman Driver of the Year — and trying to put him out of sight, out of mind.

His car was gorgeous. It had compound curves coming

back from the radiator, rivets down the sides. I even thought the bright-red paint job was a cheater — it just looked that much better than everyone else's.

The first race was at Laguna. I didn't even see him in the mirrors, and then he was beside me. I couldn't see how he'd come from that far back. He passed me and didn't look

McRae fools around

back. Every time we hit the hairpin, he powered away.

The last race was at Riverside. When Brett, the only other driver in contention, crashed on the first lap, McRae clinched the championship. I was second in the points, never winning a race.

For me, Riverside was a fitting end to the season. I thought I was headed for a big win, having led throughout, when a yellow flag waved as I was approaching the last turn of the last lap. I backed off, and Brian Redman blasted past me for the win. I went to protest, certain I had a solid case. The chief steward asked Brian whether he'd seen the flag. Brian said he hadn't. The steward said they would penalize

"Hot Lips"

Posey and M ★ A ★ S ★ H

'Tis a rare moment indeed when the ever popular, ever talking Samuel Felton Posey finds himself upstaged and we felt this picture, despite it being in the best tradition of pre-race press release photos, was worth bringing into your homes. At Riverside in preparation for the Continental next weekend, Posey was surrounded by cast members from the new TV show M.A.S.H.

Brian $250, but the win would stand. Brian later told me, smiling like the Cheshire Cat, that the steward was from his hometown of Burnley, Lancashire.

The race wasn't a total loss. "Hot Lips" Hoolihan from M*A*S*H was there, doing publicity for the show, and I got to kiss her in winner's circle.

For the next year, we made a deal with McRae to join our team and work with Jack on the car. Everything promised a great season, but our engine program was a disaster. We finished maybe half the races.

Busy weekend
Races 1,200 miles apart

In the middle of the summer of 1972, I had two races on the same weekend: the Pocono 500 and the Formula 5000 race at Donnybrooke. I was driving the Eagle from Indy at Pocono and the Surtees TS11 at Donnybrooke. Qualifying at Pocono was Thursday, the race on Saturday. Qualifying at Donnybrooke was Friday, the race on Sunday. Donnybrooke was in Brainerd, Minnesota, and Pocono in Pennsylvania. I guess I'd always wanted to have one of those complicated itineraries that lends a sense of importance to you and what you're doing.

Pocono was a tri-oval, 2.5 miles. Off the front straight, you went into a tight banked turn. The second turn came out into a tunnel with a bump that really shook up the car, so that you had to be in the right position when you hit the bump on the exit. Turn three was big, open, flat. I came into the pits after the warm-up and described the course to Jack. He asked about the fourth turn, leaving me momentarily stumped.

We had a twin-engine plane and two pilots. I qualified at Pocono and flew overnight to Brainerd, sleeping on the floor of the plane, qualified there, and went back to Pocono for the race.

Since Indy, more people had Eagles, so I didn't have quite the same edge. Here I am with Gary Bettenhausen (#7) and Salt Walther (#77). I finished sixth and won rookie of the year. The prize was a ring — triangular, a model of the track, a gold setting in a mauve band. Ellen thought it was hideous. We returned to Brainerd.

Brainerd Daily Dispatch (Minn.), Wednesday, July 26, 1972 13

SAM POSEY

★ ★ ★   ★ ★ ★   ★ ★ ★

Posey at Pocono, Then Will Fly to Donnybrooke

While the more than 30 L&M Continental Championship road racers are finely tuning their powerful machines in preparation for Sunday's (July 30) race over the 3-mile Donnybrooke circuit, Sam Posey's Winston Delta Tires Surtees will be sitting idle.

Posey, currently second in the L&M series standings, will be more than a thousand miles distant and running his Norris Eagle in the Pocono 500 Saturday, July 29.

Graham McRae has proved to be the most consistent in early running.

Sam Winston, sponsor of the Winston Delta Tires team, feels that the pendulum is now swinging to favor his team. "There can be no doubt we have made steady and strong progress in building a winner. McRae's advantage that he gained by running the Tasman Series has been

nearly overcome and we feel Donnybrooke will prove the point."

As is usually the case, Sam Posey had the final words on the Winston Delta Donnybrooke entry. "We've had a crash, an engine failure and two seconds so far this season and, quite frankly, I'm intending to see to it that all 'Cassius' McRae sees of me at Donnybrooke are my tail pipes."

The town is memorable for a huge statue of Paul Bunyan at a major intersection. The track was less distinctive, but I was happy to be back in the Surtees and not struggling with the unfamiliar and very dangerous high-speed ovals. In this shot, I'm pursued by John Cannon, Graham McRae, and Tony Settember.

I wasn't having my best day, but the car ran well and I finished third. On the cool-off lap, a course worker came running up to me with a bottle. Exhausted and thirsty, I took a few long pulls before realizing it was Schnapps. By the

time I reached victory circle, the Schnapps was kicking in, and I then thought it would be appropriate to drink as much of the Champagne as I was offered. I don't remember much from there on, but to borrow a memorable line from Tom McGuane, the night wrote a check the morning couldn't cash.

A few weeks later, someone broke into my apartment in Capistrano. The robber took nothing but the ring I'd won at Pocono. When I claimed the loss for insurance, at first no one knew what to say the ring was worth. I found it valued in the race program at $5,000, and the insurance paid.

Vasek Polak
Can-Am, Laguna Seca, 1972

Vasek Polak was a Porsche dealer who had the reputation for being number one in Porsche sales in California. He always maintained a racing team. I knew who he was, but we'd never said more than a polite hello. One day he called me up with the offer to drive the Can-Am at Laguna Seca in an open-cockpit McLaren that Jo Siffert had driven in a European version of the series.

I felt some awe in the presence of Polak. From what I knew, he started with nothing in Poland, earned everything he had, and put most of it back into the sport. He was a hero to those who knew him. I had no idea why of all the possible drivers he'd chosen me.

Milt Minter, who was running the whole season, was in Polak's first car. Next to it, mine looked a little old and shabby. Minter had been finishing in the top three or four in many of the races. I wasn't confident about my prospects. But you get in the car and want to go fast in it, and it happened that the two-year-old Porsche was built for Laguna. I was close to Minter in qualifying.

Toward the end of the race, I was running fourth, Milt just behind me. He needed the points for the championship; he wasn't going to win it, but they paid significant bonuses for where you finished. Vasek walked out to the pit wall and gave me the signal to let Minter by. I didn't hesitate to do it, although I did it on the front straight, pulling way over, so everyone could see it wasn't a real pass.

Vasek had nothing to explain to me, but he must have appreciated that a fourth place in the Can-Am was difficult to give up. Before I got out of the car, he came running up to me with a check for the prize money for fourth.

Chuck Parsons behind

Peter Gregg and the stuck seat
Lime Rock, Porsche 911, 1973

Peter Gregg arrived on the racing scene straight from Harvard and possessing an air of superiority that some found off-putting. He had a Porsche that his mechanic Jack Atkinson prepared with consummate expertise and gusto.

Peter kept you guessing as to what he was. A great driver? He had the results. An innovator in how to approach racing? He won a number of races on his tactics alone.

The color photo shows us after driving a Porsche 911

SHARON'S SAM POSEY looks pensive before the start of Saturday's Schaeffer Trans-Am race at Lime Rock. Posey, teamed with Peter Gregg, driving the Porsche Carrera in the background, finished second to Milt Minter by three-tenths of a second. Fisherpix

together in a four-hour race at Sebring in 1967, where we won our class despite a failing clutch and gearbox. By 1973, Peter had firmly established his reputation. He'd won the last eight races in that year's IMSA season. Hurley Haywood was his regular co-driver, but I had special knowledge of Lime Rock, a track where that knowledge can make a particular difference. We'd won there together before in the SCCA. Peter offered me the ride.

It was a two-hour race. He drove the first half and came in with a big lead. I was six inches taller than he was, and getting out, he thought to push the seat all the way back. As I left the pits, I tried to adjust it, but it had jammed at the back of its track. I had to decide whether to stop and try to fix it or keep going. We were far enough ahead that I thought I could win even if I was a little off the pace.

Every time I went to shift, I had to slide forward so I could reach the pedals, and then I would push back to steer. Lime Rock is a short track, and I was always in traffic. We had no radios, so I couldn't tell anyone in the pits what was wrong. They must have thought I was out for a Sunday drive; yes, I was slow, but we had the big lead.

Last lap — I was coming out of turn one and setting up for the esses when a white Porsche closed in behind me. I thought it was Milt Minter unlapping himself. I gave him room to come by. As I entered the esses, I saw a surge from the crowd on the hillside. For a second time, I'd let

Minter by in sight of the finish, this time for the lead. For the rest of the lap, I tried and failed to repass him.

The victory ceremonies were agonizing. Worst was knowing how I'd let Peter down. He would go on to win another six or seven races afterward; our second was the only break in his streak. It was typical of his realist demeanor not to make too much of it, to understand that the situation was a fluke, a gracious attitude that made my failure more conspicuous.

English conspiracy?
Tasman series, Invercargill, 1973

It was the fourth race of the 1973 Tasman in New Zealand, at Invercargill, the southernmost point of the country — near the track was a sign with the mileage to the South Pole. I had gone winless through the first three races of the four. My excuses were our Goodyear tires, which didn't work very well, and the limited pre-race practice; the locals knew the tracks already, and I was still figuring out the gearing in qualifying. But we had some Firestone rain tires, famous for their superiority, and at Invercargill it rained throughout.

I was leading near the end when I got a flat. Jack was prepared with spares mounted, but when I came back out, I was 20 seconds behind the Englishman Alan Rollinson. With five laps to go, I could see him ahead through the spray. Then out came the checkered flag. The officials all happened to be English. First Brian Redman at Riverside, and now this... I stormed up to them for an explanation, and they told me that it was too dangerous to continue the race, even though the rain had been falling from the start and had in fact lightened up a bit. Maybe if John Whitman had been there, he could have won my case.

Can-Am Ferrari
Watkins Glen, 1974

This was the only Ferrari in the world built for the Can-Am. Luigi Chinetti offered me the ride at Watkins Glen.

The first time I sat in the car, the 712 M, was as I went out for the first practice. Chinetti treated the car as just another Ferrari, but it was potentially the fastest one they'd ever built. I went to brake for the turn at the end of the back straight, and the throttle stayed on. I hit everything I could on the dash to kill the engine, to no effect. Then the throttle unstuck on its own. I finished the lap and went into the pits, but they couldn't find anything wrong and sent me back out. The next lap, the same thing happened.

Around the carbs was a ridge where the throttle linkage was exposed. At a certain speed, the air pressing down on the rear deck made it flex so that it hooked the ring on the throttle linkage. But of course when I arrived at the pits and they took off the tail section, they didn't see the problem; it was on the bodywork they'd just removed. I can't remember how someone finally figured it out.

By then, practice was coming to an end. I was determined to get in one good lap. The timers were in the first turn. I got a good run into it, leaving the braking as late as I dared. The pedal was very stiff. I jumped on it, the pressure gave way, and I mashed my toes when the pedal hit the floor.

The next day was a Formula 5000 race. The doctor gave me a cortisone shot between each toe, saying it would last half the race. I was running third or fourth when the pain returned. I couldn't make myself push the brake hard enough.

The steering column went between the pedals, so I couldn't use the other foot. I drove a tepid second half of the race, finishing way back.

The Can-Am was Sunday, and I wasn't going to be able to drive. Brian Redman took the ride and finished second. The best I would ever finish in a Can-Am was fourth.

Factory driver
Sebring 12 Hours, 1975

International Management Group, my agents, had a contact with the BMW factory team. They realized the team was going to race in America in 1975, and they thought BMW might be interested in an American driver. In November of 1974, I was in Phoenix doing an Indycar race with my Formula 5000 car. Everyone had 700 horsepower and we had 500. It was obvious from the beginning that it wouldn't go well.

After the race, IMG called me and said BMW was considering me for the team. At the time, I didn't grasp what a big opportunity it was. They would hold a test for me at Kyalami in South Africa, the day before their race there, a six-hour event. I got on a plane to Johannesburg that night, with a stopover where Muhammad Ali had his fight in Zaire. The approach was over the jungles and then into a clearing around the runway with everything a rusty red of bare earth, like clay. When we landed, they sequestered us about 50 feet from the plane, in a little room short on seats — I wound up on the floor. We took off again and made the final leg to Johannesburg.

There the reception was more lavish. A representative from BMW met me at the airport and took me to the Kyalami Ranch Hotel, where the team was staying. He told me he would pick me up in the morning for my test. They already had Ronnie Peterson and Jody Scheckter. The question was whether I could keep up well enough to fill the spot of the desired American.

SAM POSEY -- USA BMW TEAM DRIVER

I rode out to the track with my suit already on. It was apartheid, and a black man was up on a scaffold painting an advertisement on one of the billboards at the track. Below him, a white man dressed entirely in white was shouting orders up at him.

The BMW 3.0CSL seemed like a smaller version of my Trans-Am car. The track suited me perfectly: medium-to-fast turns, no hairpins. Peter Revson had been killed there earlier in the year, testing a Formula One Shadow. I had thought of him back at the hotel, but now I didn't have the chance. I did ten laps, and one matched Peterson's time and bettered Scheckter's. Jochen Neerpasch, the team manager, was there. Two or three other top executives at BMW were also involved in the team. Neerpasch called one of them and offered me the ride. By the next morning, for the race, they already had my name on the roof of the car. Ronnie started,

The team brought two cars to Sebring. Allan Moffat and Brian Redman were driving one, Hans Stuck and I the other. Just a few years earlier, the race was between the Ferrari 512s and the Porsche 917s. But the cars were so expensive, and so far from anything people could drive on the street, that the series had changed the rules. Now our sedan was a contender for the overall win, our chief rivals the Porsche 911s. But the competition was just as stiff, just at a lower speed, which you don't really notice when you're driving.

Hans started our car. I think I drove it once before we broke down.

Meanwhile, Brian had turned the other car over to Moffat. Allan was a great driver, but for whatever reason, he was having an off day. With its history, Sebring meant something back in Munich that Daytona didn't. Neerpasch decided to split Moffat's stints between Hans and me.

I believe I had a critical but not fully appreciated part in our win. As I was coming out of the pits for my first stint, Peter Gregg was in my mirrors, about to put a lap on us. I knew he would try an aggressive move at the first opportunity. I ran deep into the first and second turns. The third turn has a rough curbing on the outside. I went in even deeper. He tried to go down the inside and shot past me, lost control, and went straight over the curb, tearing up the underside of his car and putting himself out of the race. The next car was ten laps behind us.

Brian was driving at the finish. With an hour to go, and now in darkness, he had an electrical problem. If you didn't come past the start/finish with your lights on, they would disqualify you. Brian only had enough juice to run the lights for about 20 seconds a lap. He used it as he passed

putting the sedan up among the prototypes with a virtuoso drive in the rain, and then the engine blew.

After the race, I went directly to Munich to wrap up the contract and meet some of the executives, and also Martin Braungart, the engineer — a great guy, full of technical savvy, as well as the winning co-driver in the 1963 Rally of Poland. They were a serious and very professional group. Ahead of their time, they had a first-class restaurant at the factory with menus showing all the nutritional information on the food.

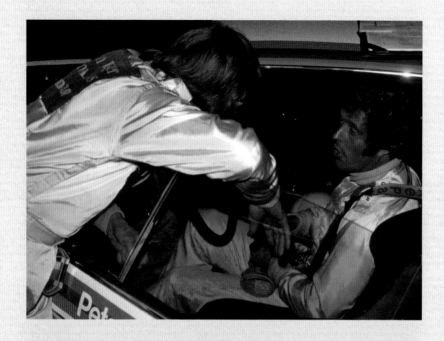

Martin Braungart

Neerpasch & Redman

John Whitman

118

the line. For the rest of the lap, he tucked in behind the nearest cars and followed their lights.

I had always felt good at Sebring. The bumps heightened the sense of speed, and you could get into an attacking mode, muscling the car around. But the track also tore cars up, and you were always afraid of breaking down. If you made it to the finish, Sebring could bring out some emotions that other tracks didn't.

The camaraderie within the team was already very strong. In the last hour, Neerpasch and I sat side by side in lawn chairs in pit lane, too tense to talk. I felt everybody in the garage willing Brian to get home.

I knew we couldn't have anyone better in the car. Brian had a great sense of how hard he could push, and he could go fast without appearing to push. Because everyone liked him so much, even opposing teams could root for him. But a couple laps from the end, he went by so slowly that I was sure he wasn't going to make it. We were also losing what had appeared to be an insurmountable lead. But then he came by again, and once more, and the race was over. It was the first victory for the team on American soil. The driver and photographer Bill Warner got this shot of winner's circle by staking his claim to one of the lighting stanchions in advance of the finish.

Harder Hall was a classic old Sebring hotel. I'd met Phil Hill in the lobby ten years earlier, going to watch the race as a kid. We were headed there to celebrate when I dropped my keys in the sand trying to unlock my door. I must have stepped on them; I knew they had to be within one or two square feet of the door, but they'd disappeared. The whole team joined me to look for them,

I'll drink to that!

A happy Brian Redman, right, gets set to take a big swig of champagne while his other winning teammates Allan Moffat, Sam Posey and Hans Stuck, from left, assist Lynn Griffis, Miss Camel GT, in getting the championship trophy on top of their winning BMW. Redman drove the winning Number 25 BMW across the finish line and go the checkered flag onl moments before. Newsphot by Sellers.

with German efficiency. It must have taken us ten minutes to find them, but if I'd had to, I would have sat out there all night sifting through the sand, smiling the whole time.

Unlike me, Hans could eat at least three quarter-pounders a meal and maintain his fighting weight. During the race, Ellen created a "Stuckburger" in his honor.

The Calder car
BMW 3.0CSL, Le Mans 24 Hours, 1975

The Calder car, as it is now known, came about in 1975 through the most improbable circumstances. Two years earlier, Braniff Airways had commissioned the famous artist Alexander Calder to paint one of their planes. Hervé Poulain, a French art auctioneer, befriended Calder and persuaded him to paint a car for Le Mans. In return for setting up this deal, Poulain would get to drive.

By the time Poulain approached BMW, several other manufacturers had already turned him down. The BMW team didn't seem like a promising candidate; they were a serious group and might have worried that the car would make them look frivolous. But the day Poulain arrived, Jochen Neerpasch happened to be in the office, and he saw an opportunity that no one else had — generating coverage in lifestyle magazines. I got the deal to drive the car because of my interest in art.

I first saw it at the press introduction at a museum in Munich. It has very bright primary colors, the same as Calder used in many of his other works. At first I didn't think the paint job related to the car as well as it could have, and also that it wouldn't stand out well from the advertising along the track. But as time has passed, I've come to admire it more and more.

Ellen and I had dinner with Poulain at his home in Paris the night before we went to the track. When we changed bottles of wine, Ellen prepared to use the same glass.

122

Nonsense, Poulain said, and threw it over his shoulder and out the window of his second-floor apartment. Poulain was a tough fit at BMW.

The car began its life as an art piece, a promotional tool. At the track, it became a racing car. Compared to the low and slinky prototypes, it didn't look to have much potential at first, but it proved unexpectedly fast.

The qualifying at Le Mans runs from six to midnight. Just before the end, I drove what I thought was the best lap I ever had at Le Mans, maybe anywhere — the ever-elusive perfect lap. On the Mulsanne, I had just enough power to catch an incredible draft from one of the prototypes. We qualified 11th. On the grid, a big box among the prototypes, the car was hard to miss.

Calder was there before the race, drunk. Everyone was pressing in to get a shot of him with the car. They would push the crowd back only for Calder to stumble out of the frame. When he was taking the obligatory photo with me, his arm draped over my shoulder, he said, "You seem like a nice young man. Can you tell me what the fuck is going on here?"

That season BMW was focused on racing in North America. The engine in our Calder car was the only one left in Europe. It had a faulty crank. Jochen knew it had about six hours in it; before the race, he'd even made us dinner reservations for that night. He told me to go as fast as I could. We were the only ones charging around with no thought about making it to the finish. The paint job had already guaranteed the car's longevity in a different sense. Hervé and I did our stints. About six hours in, Jean Guichet, the 1964 Le Mans winner, was at the wheel when the crank broke.

Alone in the desert
Baja, 1975

Seven years after my ill-fated first Baja, I got another chance. This time I was to write an article about the race for *Road & Track*. We wound up with more material than I might have hoped.

At first, our program looked more promising than the last. We had two experienced off-road drivers, Cam Warren and Tom Bryant, and a heavily modified Jeepster Commando nicknamed Holy Toledo. It was prepared by a garage in California and had finished the Baja before.

Cam and I were to start the race; Tom and John Dinkel, editors at *Road & Track*, would finish. We estimated my stint with Cam at around 15 hours. But right away, we had to stop to fix some toe-in. Then we had engine trouble — another hour lost — and a flat tire. Sometime in the night, we passed the charred remains of a flipped buggy, a grim omen.

Fine grains of sand blew into the open cockpit, and I couldn't drive without the visor on my helmet. But every minute or so, sand would cover the outside, while the inside fogged up. After flipping up the visor to wipe the underside, I would have to shut it to wipe the outside; this cycle went on for a few hours.

That year, the course ran down and back along the peninsula, starting and ending in

Ensenada. We were still on the downward leg when the winners were finishing. Cam took over during the night. He had a plan to skirt some silt beds where it was easy to get stuck. But our odometer was broken, and he would have to find the turn onto his route by eye. We got lost looking for it and then found ourselves back on the course but going the wrong way. We turned around, and Cam

TO SAN DIEGO
START - 9AM THURSDAY
SAM & CAM DRIVING
HOLY TOLEDO
ENSENADA
PAVED ROAD
PINE FOREST
60mi
89mi
HOLY TOLEDO'S
BAJA
ADVENTURE
CHECKPOINT SIX
CHECKPOINT ONE NOON THURSDAY
72mi
112mi
FINAL RESCUE 4PM SUNDAY
SAN FELIPE $150 TOWTRUCK
SAN TELMO FIX TOE-IN
CHECKPOINT FIVE
COLONIA GUERRERO
ENGINE TROUBLE LOSE ONE HOUR
SAN QUINTIN
JOHN GOES FOR HELP AT DAWN ON SATURDAY. HE RETURNS 1 AM SUNDAY
CHECKPOINT TWO DUSK THURSDAY
NIGHT FALLS
PUERTECITOS
133mi
FLAT TIRE
BREAKDOWN DUSK FRIDAY TOM BEGINS 33 HR. VIGIL
ARENOSO AIRSTRIP
WRECKED BUGGY
BOOJUM FOREST
PACIFIC OCEAN
CHECKPOINT THREE SANTA INES 11PM THURSDAY
170mi
LOW CLOUDS
PAVED ROAD
CHECKPOINT FOUR
STUCK IN SILT DAWN FRIDAY
165mi
11 AM FRIDAY TOM & JOHN TAKE OVER
404
HOLY TOLEDO
ILLUSTRATION BY THE AUTHOR

decided to risk the silt. We got stuck in a trench around dawn. Cam set out to search for help before it got any hotter.

As I waited alone with the car, my mind began to play tricks on me. I thought I heard strange noises and saw a flock of giant brown birds about 50 feet away. I wrote a note to Ellen telling her I loved her. A few hours later, a man crewing for his son found me. He lent me his shovel, and grateful for the help, I attacked the sand. We slid some boards under the tires and extricated the car just before Cam returned with another tow truck. I didn't tell him about my vision of the birds.

By then we had about three hours before the checkpoint at half distance closed at noon and we would be disqualified. To my great relief, Tom and John took over a little before. They made the checkpoint with two minutes to spare. In retrospect, maybe it would have been better if they hadn't.

Cam and I had dinner and went out in the dark to await them at the finish. But they had broken down around dusk. By the afternoon of the next day, they were still missing. We arranged for an air search to begin at dawn the following morning. I was worried for Tom and John and not at all anxious to return to the course myself in the search plane. Late that night, another plane sent out by the race organizers spotted the jeep. Tom and John were finally rescued the next afternoon, after over 30 hours stranded in the desert.

Back in California, as Cam and I were telling the story, I found out that he also thought he'd seen the birds and also hesitated to mention them. In fact, it turned out that a species of giant bird similar to the Hawaiian Nene was indigenous to that area.

For the article I drew a map of our run.

Night at Le Mans
BMW 3.0CSL, 1976

In 1976, Jochen Neerpasch got me another ride with BMW at Le Mans, with Harald Grohs and Hughes de Fierlant. We finished 10th. I had a deal with *Sports Illustrated* to write an article about the race. As soon as my stint ended, I would dictate my mental notes to Ellen in the pits. The Mulsanne at night, I thought, was like driving down a dark hall at 185 mph. I wrote the article from Ellen's notes, the magazine ran it, and later, out of the blue, *Reader's Digest* offered to buy it for a staggering price. I did better from the article than from driving in the race.

ILLUSTRATION BY ROBERT HEINDEL

DOWN A DARK HALL AT 185 MPH

Bone-weary and alone, the men who race at Le Mans must hurtle through a night that they fear will never end

by SAM POSEY

The 24-hour race at Le Mans is a monument to the idea that life goes on. It is a French national institution dating back more than half a century, with a quarter of a million devotees turning out every June for a scene that perhaps can be compared only to the Woodstock rock festival. But to the driver, speeding through the night portion of the race in a vehicle that is about as sturdy as an eggshell, with lights as useful at 200 mph as miner's lamps, the idea that life will go on—or that the night will ever end—doesn't seem the least bit assured.

At any time, day or night, Le Mans is an imposing circuit. Its many fast turns permit laps of an extremely high average speed but, because the track is narrow and lined with guardrails, the sensation is of aiming your car down a twisting hallway. A lap is 8.36 miles long and takes you through the rural country-side on the outskirts of the railhead town of Le Mans, 135 miles southwest of Paris. Most of the circuit consists of main roads ordinarily open for public use, and as you rip past fields and farmhouses and occasionally plunge through dense pine forests you are in fact rushing from one small Le Mans suburb to another. Mulsanne is one of these towns. Arnage is another. At racing speeds, however, you rarely notice the scenery.

At night there's almost nothing to see except the road. Cars are no longer recognizable by their shapes or colors; they are just twin dots of light. The few illuminated landmarks that do exist surge at you out of the dark in an endless repetitive sequence. The pits. The carnival at the esses. The café that's one-third of the way along the straight leading from Le Mans out to Mulsanne. The rest of the lap becomes abstract; rows of bright reflectors along both sides of the road outline the route clearly but make it look more like a lighted diagram than a race circuit. In this way the night conceals many of the specific hazards of the course, replacing a sense of coming and going from particular danger points with a pervasive uneasiness.

Half of a Le Mans driver's night is spent on the track, the other half trying to get some sleep while his co-driver is out with the car. The more organized teams rent trailers behind the pits as dormitories for their drivers, and in the eight years I have done the race I have always gone to my trailer knowing I must sleep to keep my reflexes working. But sleep has never been easy to come by.

In the darkness of the trailer I see images of the road rushing at me, as if all those laps have been stamped on my mind, a tape loop that cannot be shut off. If I close my eyes, a second later I'm grabbing for the edge of the cot, convinced I'm falling; hours of violent motion in a car have upset my balance. Every year the trailer walls seem thinner, or else the cars are louder, and the roaring is a reminder that my car is out there somewhere. When I am particularly tired I get the idea that the car is still going not so much because the nuts and bolts are right but because the whole team is willing it to run—sheer mind over matter. For me to sleep is to reduce by one the force that keeps the car going.

One year, 1970, I spent my hours in the trailer half convinced I would not live through the night. That was the year it rained for 20 of the 24 hours. Rain is frightening even on a slow track in broad daylight. At night, driving through Le Mans' fast turns and down the long Mulsanne straight, it is terrifying. On the water-soaked track the tires of my Ferrari aquaplaned uncontrollably, the steering wheel sometimes being wrenched back and forth in my hands and sometimes going dead. Seen from the cockpit the rain didn't fall; it came at me horizontally. Drivers usually remain at the
continued

A first-class team
Mirage GR8, Le Mans 24 Hours, 1977

Harley Cluxton, in my view, had always been a star. He was in his early 20s when I met him, running errands for the NART team. He just wanted to be around racing, but he was more than an enthusiast. His father had a very successful law practice, and Harley, who was Harley Cluxton III, became a lawyer too — and also, at 26, the youngest

authorized Ferrari dealer in the US. He never tried to make himself the center of attention, but from years out, he was working to achieve his dream of running his own team.

In 1976, he took over the Le Mans-winning Gulf Mirage team when John Wyer retired, retaining the renowned engineer John Horsman. Le Mans was the passion and the

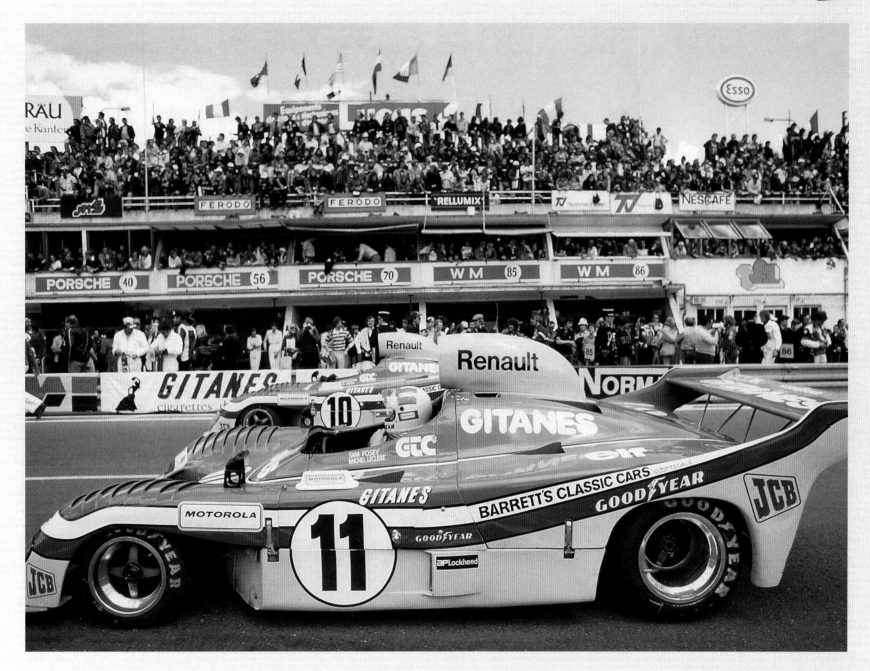

focus of the team each year, and they took every detail into account in preparing for the race. For 1977, Harley had two cars. Jean-Pierre Jarier and Vern Schuppan would drive one, Michel Leclère and I the other.

Harley did everything first class, which at Le Mans meant the Hôtel de France. Ellen and I had a room overlooking a classic French garden. Practice went until midnight, and then you had half an hour of fast driving back to the hotel, where the restaurant stayed open until 2 a.m.

In the race, Leclère and I broke down early. Schuppan and Jarier were second. In the last hour, a cylinder failed on the leading Porsche, and it looked as if the car might not make it to the finish. As I pulled for our team to inherit the win, I also had to admit to agonizing over the thought of not being the winning driver on the winning team.

With Harley Cluxton

My last Le Mans
Mirage GR8, 1978

In 1978, Harley Cluxton gave me one more shot. After the team's second place the year before, we believed we could win. But the first time down the Mulsanne in practice, the buffeting from the wind was so bad I could hardly see. We'd had a 24-hour test at Phoenix a few months before and hadn't had the problem, but the higher speeds on the Mulsanne must have made the difference. Michel Leclère and I, as the tallest, thought we had the worst of it. Even John Horsman couldn't figure it out. In the photo to the right, Jacques Lafitte describes the effect, to Harley's amusement.

John Horsman

134

In the race, our car broke down before I got in. I switched to the other car with Laffite and Vern Schuppan.

I remember standing in the pits just after dawn as the second car was undergoing repairs. Harley came around and said to the three of us, "Gentlemen, the car is ready. I wonder whether one of you would get in it." Each of us looked at the others. Harley had hired me for an outrageous sum, and we went back many years. I said I would do four or five laps while he and the other guys figured out what to do next.

Laffite and Schuppan took over for the rest of the race and made it to the finish, in 10th. It felt like a celebration with so many of my friends and family there; I was just sorry we hadn't done better. It was my last Le Mans.

Concorde commute
Monaco to Lime Rock, 1979

The idea was that I would go to Monaco to cover the grand prix for ABC and race a Datsun 260Z for Bob Sharp at Lime Rock the next day. We were doing the grand prix on tape delay, so we stayed to work on the show until late into the night. I got back to my room in the early morning. My flight from Nice, the closest airport to Monaco, was only a few hours off; too nervous to sleep, I paced around the room until I had to go. At checkout, my bill included a heavy charge for drinks on the patio the previous afternoon, when I'd been in the ABC trailer. I protested the charge, and they canceled it, but it seemed like an inauspicious beginning to the trip.

In Nice, bad weather delayed the flight to Paris, where I had a connection to the Concorde. They were shutting the door as I ran down the jetway, but I made it.

AIR FRANCE

Dear Concorde Passenger:

Welcome to the exclusive society of supersonic travel.

Recently while aboard the Air France Concorde, you and your fellow passengers flew faster than the speed of sound. The SOUND BARRIER CERTIFICATE enclosed testifies to and authenticates this unique achievement.

We trust that your trip on Concorde in every way reflected the care and concern that we of AIR FRANCE always devote to make intercontinental travel a truly extraordinary experience.

Congratulations and Welcome again to Air France's New World of Flying.

Cordially,

Roland J. Hawkins
General Manager, USA

SPORT

Turbo Lag Out, Jet Lag In

• Lime Rock's long-standing ban on Sunday racing enables some of the more active IMSA participants to indulge in a little moonlighting on the long Memorial Day weekend. They bail out to take part in other Sunday events, then rush back to be on time for the IMSA finals on Monday. This year the antics reached a whole new dimension.

At the entry level to the jet set, timer-scorer Judy Stropus zipped over to Bryar, New Hampshire, for a quick run at some SCCA national points in her Showroom Stock Monza.

More complicated was David Hobbs' schedule, which had him in Charlotte for the taping of the World 600 for CBS.

"We finished qualifying the McLaren BMW Turbo here at 4:20 p.m. on Saturday, with me on the pole—the timekeeper got it wrong," he noted with a slightly sarcastic twist. "Then we drove to Hartford and flew to Charlotte. I said hi and bye Sunday on the telly, drove to the airport, caught the plane at 8:30 p.m. to Hartford, drove from Hartford to nearby Sharon, and got in about midnight." In the rain-soaked Winston GT, Hobbs finished second to Peter Gregg's Porsche 935.

Sam Posey's itinerary was considerably

more complicated. He, like Hobbs, was doing television commentary. But Posey was doing it for ABC in Monte Carlo. After his usual razzle-dazzle verbal performance during the Grand Prix, his journey across the ocean began.

"From Monte Carlo we drove over to Nice, which is not a long drive, and then we were on a plane from Nice to Paris, and we left at 11:00 a.m. from Paris on the Concorde.

"We got in at 8:45 a.m. on the dot at JFK. Air France had a guy who took me through customs. I had carry-on luggage and walked through to a man who took me over to where a helicopter was waiting, which flew me to my house in Sharon. Jim Haynes (the Lime Rock general manager) was nice enough to give me a police escort to the track, and I arrived at the exact moment of warmup practice for the GTU cars."

What Posey didn't mention is the 45 hours he went without any real sleep. Having missed qualifying, he started his Datsun Z-car last on the grid of the GTU race. He also won.

"We may never let him qualify again," bubbled team owner Bob Sharp.

—Glenn Howell

Continued

137

At Lime Rock

Tired Posey wins car race

By PAUL SELEMAN

LIME ROCK — Sam Posey was so happy Monday that, for a few moments at least, he forgot how exhausted he was.

You see, it was like this for Sam Posey this Memorial Day weekend.

He started the holiday in Monaco, doing television commentary for the Grand Prix of Monaco. After the race was over late Sunday afternoon, he left on an airplane bound for Paris.

From there, he boarded a Concorde Jet for the transatlantic flight to New York, arriving at Kennedy Airport at 8:45 a.m. yesterday.

Twenty-five minutes later, he's in a helicopter that takes him to his mother's home in Sharon where he jumps into a car and drives — with considerable energy — to nearby Lime Rock Park, getting there with just enough time to suit up and take a few practice laps in the Datsun Z he is to pilot in the 75-mile Winston GTU race.

Then he had about an hour to collect himself as best he could before starting from the very last spot in the field of 18 be-

drove his Porsche to an overwhelming victory, finishing a lap plus 42.7 seconds ahead of Hobbs, his nearest challenger.

The inaugural 75-mile Kelly Girl Challenge was a two-car duel between Gene Felton and Jerry Thompson until lap 27 when Thompson bowed out with engine failure. Felton, driving a Skylark, went on to win the 49-lap race by 18.51 seconds over Pat Bedard, the editor of Car and Driver Magazine.

Rob McFarlin, in a Datsun 200SX, captured the 100-mile Champion Spark Plug Challenge by 32.3 seconds over Roger Mandeville.

A crowd in excess of 25,000 watched the action, many of them even staying when the drizzle began to resemble a downpour.

TOP THREE FINISHERS
Winston GTU

1. Sam Posey, Sharon, Conn., Datsun Z; 2. Don Devendorf, Los Angeles, Calif., Datsun ZX; 3. Jim Fitzgerald, Clemmons, N.C., Datsun ZX. Race time: 48:05.78. Average speed: 93.54 mph.

Kelly Girl Challenge
Gene Felton, Atlanta, Ga., Skylark; 2. Pat Bedard, New York, N.Y....

In New York three hours later, a representative of Air France rushed me through customs and out of the terminal. My friend Don Carberry had made the two-hour trip from Sharon to drive me five minutes from the terminal to JFK's helipad, saving me a potentially disastrous delay in the taxi line.

Here all my carefully laid plans again almost came apart. The pilot didn't know where Lime Rock was, and I'd forgotten to send him directions. Instead of taking the nap I'd planned, I guided us using familiar roads. We landed on the lawn at my mother's house, where a police escort was waiting to bring me to the track. At seven and a half hours, I believe the trip was a record — one that with the retirement of the Concorde might now be hard to beat.

I expected the race to be an anticlimax. Not having qualified, I was starting at the back of a 25-car field. But the car was handling beautifully; I gained about seven places in the first turn and picked my way up to fifth without ever getting held up. I assumed the leader, Don Devendorf, would be far up the road by then, but he was having engine problems and had stacked up the field behind him. I finished the last third of the race in the lead.

Sometime later, I learned that a friend of a friend knew I was staying at the hotel in Monaco and figured he might as well charge his drinks to my room.

Finishing the Baja
Frank Vessels, Chevy Blazer, 1980

For my third and last Baja, in 1980, everything seemed to fall into place. That year, the race was again a loop beginning and ending in Ensenada, which made it better for TV coverage, and ABC had the deal. I was to ride with Frank "Scoop" Vessels, a real pro with several Bajas behind him and a favorite to win his class in his Chevy Blazer. He was also a very successful breeder of American quarter horses; his grandfather had founded the track at Los Alamitos. The only liability from my standpoint was that a race for the win could be its own terrifying ride, especially for someone with my still limited off-road experience.

I rode with Frank from the start to the first checkpoint — a trip of about two hours — and set off from there to begin a day of filming in one of ABC's helicopters, in coordination with Jackie Stewart, who had a second helicopter. It was illegal in Mexico to fly them after dusk, so my pilot had to leave me on the course with about 150 miles to go. I was planning to ride with Frank to the finish, where Ellen was waiting along with Jim McKay, so that I could deliver a firsthand account for the show. Jim was doing his part from the ABC compound — no fool.

When I went to get into the car, Frank tried to talk me out of it; he was having trouble with his brakes and wanted his mechanic aboard. But I insisted — on the face of it, because of my deal with ABC, but also from my desire not to be stranded 150 miles from the finish, in the dark.

Frank was leading his class but believed someone was closing in. Vague information of this kind was typical of the Baja. He had no rearview mirror and kept looking over his shoulder. Approaching Ensenada, we entered a fog bank so dense that he had to slow to around 30 mph. We feared all the time that this mythic pursuer would emerge from the fog behind us and pass us for the win. Early that morning, Frank had been loose, relaxed. Now he was exhausted, barely hanging on. The last few miles were downhill through a series of hairpins. We had two gears — high and low — and Frank shifted between them what seemed to be every few seconds. In the final few miles, the tension was relentless. Then we came around a corner and bright lights appeared right in front of us. It was the finish. They would

World of Sports program being filmed before and during the event. The international road racer is known for his sometimes blunt comments on the world of motorsport, but this trip Posey was truly excited about the Blazer ride in Baja. "The first time I raced in the Baja 1000 in 1968," Posey recalled, "it was in a two-seat buggy with a streamlined body and a wing. The leading edge of the wing served as an air intake, which was rather clever, but I don't

remarks on off roading from the right seat in practice were tempered with a bit of awe. Sam said that it seemed so incredible to be able to go so fast over such rough terrain,

to the checkered flag in the dense fog that shrouded the piney woods and the mountain pass.

The joy in victory was real, as real for Sam as for Frank,

have felt more comfortable driving himself, Sam remarked with modesty that he didn't think so. He didn't think he could have driven as fast or with the confidence that Frank did, but maybe someday, with a lot more practice, he might try driving. Hours later Posey was still bubbling with enthusiasm about the Blazer ride, and his Blazer tales will be a definite part of the ABC-TV show this winter.

—*Jean Calvin*

PHOTOS BY ELLEN GRIESEDIECK

Can A Pavement Racer Thrive Off Road? Sam Posey Did

Frank Vessels talks to ABC's Jim McKay, while Sam Posey looks on.

turn on all the lights for a theatrical effect when an important contender was coming in.

The next thing I knew, Jim McKay was interviewing me, Ellen beside him, and friends of Frank's were gathering around him with congratulations; he'd won the class and was third overall. In all the hazards of the trip, he'd never as much as dented the car.

For my part, I had finally seen the finish and the race from the point of view of a winner. I was full of admiration for it all. Did I want to do it again? Maybe three times was enough.

Racing with Paul Newman
Datsun 280ZX, 1980

When Bob Sharp stopped racing, he hired me to take his place co-driving with Paul Newman. The car, a Datsun designed by Trevor Harris, arrived late. We couldn't find an open track near enough to test. Because of Paul, Stewart Airforce Base in New York opened up a runway for us. It was the first time anyone had driven the car.

Ellen was there taking pictures for an article for *Sports Illustrated*. We had to drive the shots to their offices in midtown Manhattan after the test. As we left, the sun was setting, the light raking across the runways. The car looked spectacular. It should have been a moment of great excitement and anticipation for the racing to come. But already we sensed the car just wasn't fast. It was too wide, too heavy, the paint job too elegant.

Paul Newman and Sam Posey eye Bob Sharp's new twin turbo V-8 Datsun Z-car at Elkhart Lake.

Bob Harmeyer

Sharp's turbo 280-ZX meets flood of protest in GT ranks

Paul and I co-drove at Atlanta and Elkhart Lake. We were never competitive with the turbo Porsches. The car was a year too late. It was a real disappointment for Paul. My career was winding down, but even though Paul was ten years older, he was still coming on. With the right car, he could have been mixing it up with the top guys.

144

Evening at Sebring
Datsun 280ZX, 1981

The days of Formula 5000 and Indy and BMW were behind me. But a man named Fred Stiff approached me saying he wanted to race and wanted me to drive for him. We asked Jack McCormack to prepare the car, a Datsun 280ZX.

In 1981, we went to Sebring for the 12 hours, staying at a fancy hotel Fred had chosen. It was the place to be if you were a spectator at the race, but it was far from the track, not very convenient if you were driving. We ate breakfast there the morning of the race. I think that was the main event for Fred. I believed he liked me and liked the idea of racing,

but maybe not so much the driving itself. He wasn't in great shape, and hoping that a lot of sugar and carbs would make up for it, he ate about five candy bars immediately before getting in the car. Out on the runways, if you miss an apex, you can find yourself in the middle of nowhere, without any points of orientation. After a section on asphalt, you pass onto the concrete of the runways, going down one, veering to the right, and starting onto another. Fred missed the right and kept going out into the night until he hit a drainage ditch a few hundred yards beyond the course. We had to bring the car in on a wrecker.

Jack McCormack was working with Keith Black to develop a turbo engine that would have produced an insane amount of horsepower for a Datsun 280ZX. The engine was about a month off when Fred ran out of money and pulled the plug on the team.

Lemon meringue
Lola T600, Elkhart Lake, 1981

Not long after Sebring, I landed at O'Hare airport in Chicago, went to a phone bank, and found a message from Brian Redman. He offered me a ride with him in the next race of the IMSA championship, at Elkhart Lake.

The car was a Lola T600. It was yellow, beautiful. Brian was virtually undefeated in it. If he was second or better in the race, he would clinch the championship.

The car was the first I'd driven with ground effect. I'd never felt that I had any edge at Elkhart Lake. The carousel is a downhill turn that goes on and on, with a bump near the end. With the ground effect, I knew I could have taken it faster. We had two days of practice. I got in four or five

	RACE TIME			LAP TIME		
12						
11	33	18	459	2	15	777
10	31	02	680	2	17	498
9	28	45	182	4	26	806
8	24	18	376	2	15	104
7	22	03	272	2	11	019
6	19	52	253	2	10	98D
5	17	41	272	2	12	663
4	15	28	609	4	51	202
3	10	37	407	2	15	070
2	8	22	337	2	16	595
1	6	05	742	2	37	55
START	3	28	587	XXXXXXXXXXX		

Driver **REDMAN / POSEY**

Fastest Lap Time 2:10.981 Speed _____

laps each time. I hadn't driven a car that good lately, if ever. I loved the car even though I knew I wasn't getting the most out of it. When the seat wasn't right for me, Brian, in his gentlemanly way, fitted it to me instead of to him. Though I was a few seconds off his pace, he expressed total confidence in me.

The day of the race was crisp, the car perfect, everything like a stage set. It was a long race, about 300 miles. Brian would start the car, I would take over, and he would finish. My part was to bring the car in undamaged at the end of my stint without losing too much time. I did that, and Brian finished second.

That night we went out to Siebkens, a pub about a mile from the track where all the teams hung out. We had a

table in the back; the mood was festive. Near the end, Brian was showing off his trick of walking around with a spoon resting on his nose. David Hobbs came up behind him, tapped him on the shoulder, and hit him in the face with a pie when he turned. Without missing a beat, Brian said, "Lemon meringue." It was wonderful to have been part of Brian's championship.

Not long before, I'd found out that Ellen was pregnant. Sometime during the dinner, I realized I was going to quit. It turned out to be my last professional race.

Ellen and I were doing an article on the race for *Road & Track*. The day afterward, she went around with Brian, lying on her back on the floor on the passenger side and getting this shot by shooting up as he drove. Then I drove her around in a rental car as fast as I could, following Brian through the carousel, while she leaned out the window shooting. She said she was more nervous riding with me in the rental.

Backwards race
Oldsmobile, Lime Rock, 1988

Sometime in the early 80s, *Road & Track* began reserving Lime Rock for a day each summer and holding entertaining events to promote the magazine. I had the idea of a backwards race — one lap of the track, from a standing start. What made it interesting was that most traditional performance cars weren't necessarily good in reverse. What you needed was a long reverse gear.

I entered a pickup truck in the inaugural event, lowering the tailgate so I could see the road, and then our Datsun station wagon the second year. Butch Sherwood, the former track manager, appeared with a backhoe, planning to "crush" the competition. John Fitch ran away with the first race; I finished a distant third. The second year, John won again. He had a dark-blue Caprice; it didn't look like much, but I found out that he'd beguiled some guys at Chevrolet into lending him the car specifically for this race. I didn't know what they'd done, but it was apparent to me that he was cheating, except that by my own decree, the event had no rules.

In July of the third year, a few weeks before the race, my phone rang. It was Oldsmobile; they were irritated about getting blown off in this important event by their rival division. They asked whether I would be interested in a car that would threaten John Fitch's dominance. I was.

As the date approached, I prepared myself as well as I could by driving backwards in my driveway in the Datsun, getting up some pretty good speed in the confined space. I started to doubt whether I could do better in the new car.

The night before the race, it arrived at the track in a transporter, from Detroit. The Oldsmobile guys kept it inside, also covered by a tarp. With a twirl of his wrist, someone revealed the machine beneath. It was a station wagon without any apparent distinction. My heart sank. But the innovation turned out to be below the skin. They'd switched the transmission — an automatic — so that I had the forward gears in reverse, and to help me deal with this extra

Limerock backup 1

IN THE sdrawkcab race (that's backwards to you non-mirror writing readers), Lime Rock local Sam Posey blew away the competition. No mean feat when you consider the competition included 2-time winner and lap record holder John Fitch and Bob Akin in his fast, fast Porsche 928S. Posey and Fitch were reversing GM products that were virtually identical except for body style and division. Posey's was an Olds Custom Cruiser station wagon; Fitch's, a Chevy Caprice 4-door. Reports that Posey's wagon had to be trailered to the track because it couldn't be driven in a forward direction were never substantiated. Sour grapes? Sophisticated cheating? With the growing popularity of this event (we had nine entries), I guess I'll have to require some form of technical inspection this year. Drivers caught cheating will be suitably castergated.

Almost forgot. In a rare reversal of form, Posey set a new sdrawkcab lap record, smashing the once-thought-untouchable 2-minute barrier with a time of 1 minute 56.63 seconds, for an average speed of 46.30 mph.

Bob Akin won the Sportsman's award . . . the hard way. As he crossed the finish line, Bob attempted to loop his Porsche in a demonstration of the old gangster U-turn. Unfortunately, it only rotated 90 degrees and then slid off the track. Bob applied the brakes, only to discover to his chagrin that the 928's anti-lock brakes prevented the car from spinning. The Porsche's rear bumper tapped the guardrail, luckily taking the force of the blow on the bumper overriders. Despite this mild set front, Bob promises to be back up to speed for this year's event.

> *R&T would like to thank the following companies for contributing prizes for the Manufacturers Challenge Cup VIII and the Backwards Race: Omega (watches), Rado (watches), Tumi (attaché cases), Polaroid (cameras), Parker (pen and pencil sets), Pirelli (books),*

PHOTOS BY JOE RUSZ

John Dinkel drops the checkered flag, starting the sdrawkcab race. Sam Posey (inset) in the Olds Custom Cruiser (foreground) was the winner, setting a new lap record of 1 minute 56.63 seconds.

horsepower, also changed the steering ratio and the front suspension to make the car more stable. I saw that I would need a test before the race. The representative from *Road & Track* let us go up on the skid pad. I went creeping up there at the maximum forward speed of 10 mph. In the dark, with the weaker reverse beams, I could hardly see. I didn't know whether the car was understeering or oversteering. With my usual lack of technical savvy, I could only describe the handling as weird.

Raceday morning, I dressed in racing shoes and a tux. Starting positions were drawn from a hat. I got a fantastic start from the second row, bursting into the lead just after the flag waved. I had no trouble through the tricky first turn or the esses. The exhilaration of my widening lead grew with each corner. Then came the uphill. Halfway up, I realized I couldn't see the road past the station wagon's huge tail. I took my bearings off the guardrail on the outside. From there on, I coasted home.

Fitch took the defeat well, saying he'd had his years of glory and now it was my turn. Chevy never knew what had hit them. They'd grown complacent and let their R&D languish. If you're not moving backwards, as the adage goes, you're falling behind.

Comeback!
Formula Ford at Lime Rock

About 35 years after I retired, Skip Barber launched a drivers' club at Lime Rock and gave me an honorary family membership — an incredible gift. For the first time since I started racing, the track was completely accessible. John and Judy, my son and daughter, had just taken the Barber three-day racing school and wanted to do more. The best and cheapest way, I thought, would be for us to buy a car of our own. I had my friend Don Breslauer to help me find it and to prepare it. I was also hoping to drive it myself. Ellen was a little anxious about the plan but let it go forward.

Don and I decided on a Formula Ford. John and Judy had just driven them in the racing school; they were light and fast — no question they were real racing cars — but also reliable and relatively safe.

Don searched the country for the right one. We found it on a rainy day in a garage less than a mile from his house. It was called a Titan. It was red with white pinstriping and the heraldic head of a Titan on the nose. It looked to me like the Formula One Lotus Jim Clark had driven when I was falling in love with the sport.

We saw the driving as something fun we could do together. But there was also a competitive aspect. I had been diagnosed with Parkinson's disease, and I couldn't run, ride a bike, or play tennis or even ping-pong with John anymore. I missed competition, and I wanted to show my kids that I could still do something behind the wheel. Both of them have a competitive streak of their own.

I didn't have much experience with Formula Fords. They were a stepping stone for many great drivers, but they became extremely popular just after I'd moved on to the next level.

Don did a perfect job of preparing the car. In two laps, it was as if the 35 years hadn't passed. I was back driving a car at Lime Rock, and confronted with all the special challenges of a lap there. It felt good to be experiencing the speed again, the control, and maybe even a little fear. Driving still triggered the same emotions, and I believed I could still do it.

Don wrote my times in a notebook and showed me when I

Don Breslauer

came in. A lap time contains so much. It's an achievement in itself and also a sign of potential, and the watch doesn't lie. My mood swung with the times just as it always had.

We had the car for three or four sessions, and then John had a serious crash in the uphill. One lap he didn't come around, and then the wrecker went out. I repeated the same logic to myself that I had in justifying the program — Formula Fords were safe cars. He might have wracked it up, but he would be fine. But a part of my mind wasn't thinking logically.

He turned out to be fine, though furious with himself for his mistake. But the crash forced me take a closer look at our program. The car was almost 50 years old. It wasn't just like the Barber School cars; it was lighter, faster, and more dangerous. Focusing on its beauty, its romantic connections, and the pleasure of driving it, I'd let myself overlook these other facts. If our program was to continue, we would have to

Don Breslauer

Clockwise from me: Judy,
Rick Bell, Don Breslauer

With John and Don Breslauer

find something more practical.

Don said it would cost more to repair the Titan than to buy a similar car in good condition. My friend Mike Rand sold us one; at the nominal price, it was more of a gift. Called a PRS, it was at least ten years newer than the Titan; it looked more like the Barber cars. Don went through it and once again made everything right. We painted it bright red with white numbers. I thought it was beautiful.

I invited John and Judy to share the driving with me again. But Judy had moved to the city and John had decided that if he made another mistake, he wanted it to be in a car of his own. Unlike the Titan, this car would be all mine.

I had a molded seat, which can make an incredible difference in the feel of a car. When I arrived in the paddock for the first session, Don had the car warmed up and ready

to go. I wanted to beat the times I'd set in the Titan.

During my career, I was switching cars from one week to the next, and it seemed important to regard them as no more than tools. But I began to develop a special feeling for this car.

At my request, after the second year, Don found someone to bore out the engine. It might have seemed like a strange request: I was spending money to improve the performance of a car that I had no plans to race against anyone else. In fact, the modified engine would make the car ineligible for its class. I can only say that I just wanted to go faster, and if I couldn't improve my technique, I could add horsepower. For a change, we also repainted the car dark green.

We asked Rick Bell, a local hotshoe and friend whose unassuming nature belies what he can do behind the wheel, to test out the new engine. He bested my best times in the

car while still warming it up and turned it over to me. I had done a few personal bests when two other drivers spun in front of me. I avoided them but hit the guardrail head on.

Walking around the pits after the crash, I was still high on adrenaline and didn't know I'd passed out in the car for a few minutes before the wrecker arrived. I hadn't remembered to take my hand off the wheel before I hit, and I'd dislocated my thumb; it wouldn't heal for a couple months.

Still, the next season, I was anxious to get back in the car, and to go faster. This time, the answer seemed to be Weber carbs. I should have remembered the misadventure with the side-draft carbs on the McLaren years ago. Don installed the Webers, and again we had Rick go out first. But the carbs kept catching fire. Both Don and Rick, who was also an accomplished mechanic, were at a loss.

Don was determined to get the car right again, and he did. Rick did some blistering laps. When I saw the times, I knew that even to approach them, I would have to take incredible risks all the way around the track. I could still do a time I was proud of, just not so proud when I saw what Rick was doing.

Somewhere between the ages of 50 and 100, Dan Gurney said, you slow down. For many years, even after I'd lost balance and coordination outside the car, Parkinson's didn't seem to affect my driving. Even on the track, where the demands were greater, the adrenaline seemed to compensate, although later I would feel more depleted than usual, as if my body had drawn down a limited reserve. But then my driving also began to decline.

One unfortunate aspect of Parkinson's is how it interacts with factors like tension so that sometimes it's hard to tell which part of the decline is you and which the disease. It also affects your ability to recognize the decline.

I drove the car a few times at what felt like a comfortable speed. In one or two sessions, with remarkable generosity from the track and the other drivers, they ended sessions early so I could go out alone. I still loved driving, loved the feel of the car. But I was ever more aware of not getting the most out of it. Finally, I had Rick drive it for me once or twice, just so I could see it in action. But being a car owner, not a driver, wasn't for me.

Don found separate buyers for the engine and the car, receiving for both the price we'd paid. The car's new owners, a father and his young son, did me the honor of asking whether they could use my number. In the end, the program had been satisfactory in every respect, except that it had to end.

Lawn Car

Before we sold the Formula Ford, I asked Don Breslauer to find something I could use to roar around on our lawn. I wanted it to be a car, not an ATV — low to the ground, with a steering wheel, not handlebars. He came up with a small dune buggy with a roll cage and knobby tires, called a Hammerhead. It has a top speed of about 25 mph, although the brochure said 40. It has stood up to crashes into a pool fence, a tree, and buried rocks, and even a three-foot jump off a stone retaining wall — at least with Don there to repair it.

Each spring, I design a course through the high grass that borders our lawn, and the landscaping crew gamely mows it. More than a few luminaries of today's driving scene have tried their hand, including actor and racer Patrick Dempsey, and Alex Gurney and his co-driver in the Daytona Prototype series, John Fogarty. Before their race at Lime Rock over Memorial Day weekend, Alex and John visited us for the Indy 500; in ad breaks, they would rush out to try and better the current record set by the other or by my son, whose light weight on the long uphill pull proved a difficult advantage to overcome. As the afternoon wore on, they began to take a closer look at the exhaust system, and Don found himself called out to tune it.

I have to believe that I'm going to get back in a car, even on the track. For too long, racing has been an essential part of me. But until then, in the lawn car, I can still get in touch with it. The course is about 200 yards from where John Whitman and I began coasting down toward the lake on our Mudge Pond Express.

Answers to quiz questions
(At the time of the quiz)

4 Identify the following designations.
There is only one car for each designation.

105E	Ford (Anglia)
GTL	Porsche
PV-544	Volvo
211	Datsun
541-R	Jensen
12-M	Taunus
RS-21	Toyopet Crown
3.2	BMW
HBR-5	Deutsch-Bonnet
S-440	Skoda
PV-444-L	Volvo
7	Austin (also Lotus)
C.N.7	Campbell's Bluebird
30	NSU Prinz
96	Saab
360	Porsche GP (Cisitalia)
17-M	Taunus
PL-17	Panhard
2-CV	Citroën
4-CV	Renault
K3	MG
T.3	Rover turbine car
122-S	Volvo
S-2	Bentley
46	Bugatti
246	Ferrari

5 Which of the following should properly be hyphenated?

Hyphenated

Ace-Bristol

Austin-Healey

Deutsch-Bonnet

Fiat-Abarth

Mercedes-Benz

Rolls-Royce

Lister-Jaguar

Not hyphenated

Alfa Romeo

Aston Martin

Auto Union

Facel Vega

Super America

Hillman Minx

14. Random Questions.

page eight

a) What to the nearest 5 hp was the power output of the Ward Lime Rock midget?

b) What three men are responsible for the Echidna?

c) What is Ugolini's first name?

d) Basically, is the GP Cooper an understeering or oversteering car?

e) Who is Jacques Washer?

f) Who is generally considered the best driver in town-to-town long-distance races, and who wore that crown before him?

g) Before the 1959 Portuguese GP, only two GP drivers had ever driven the Monsanto circuit before. Who were they?

h) When & where did Gendebien first drive in a championship Grand Epreuve?

i) What is meant by the "Gran Premio Nuvolari"?

j) Who was known as Oberingenieur?

k) Who is responsible for Lola? Sting Ray?

l) What was the smallest (engine displacement) car ever to win Le Mans?

m) Name two double & two triple winners at Le Mans.

n) At what famous GP did Nuvolari attempt to steer a burning car with his legs?

o) What was the "famous pitstop where everything went wrong?

p) What driver lost an ear and had a (over to next)

---

14 Random questions:

a) 170 hp

b) John Staver, Ed Grierson, and Bill Larson

c) Nello

d) Understeering

e) Gendebien's co-driver (and cousin)

f) Gendebien, Taruffi

g) Hill, Gregory

h) Jan. '56, Buenos Aires

i) Mantua, Nuvolari's birthplace

j) Neubauer, dumpkopf

k) Eric Broadley, Allan Ross, Bill Mitchell

l) Chinetti's 2-liter Ferrari, 1949

m) Triple winners: Barnato ('28, '29, '30), Chinetti ('32, '34, '49), Hill ('58, '60, '61), Gendebien ('58, '60, '61); double winners: Flockhart ('56, '57), Bueb ('55, '57), Birkin ('29, '31), Sommer ('32, '33), Wimille ('37, '39)

n) Monaco 1931

o) Nuvolari '35 at the Ring

p) Behra (if you guessed it from this incomplete clue, congratulations!)

Alfred Neubauer (good appetite)

Jean Behra (false ear)

Thank you

First, I'd like to thank Bob D'Amato for coming up with this book and for his own interest in reliving my experiences. It was worth it for me for the Saturdays we spent remembering the stories and looking at the photos. My longtime friend Judy Stropus pointed us toward Evro, our publishers; a pleasure to work with from start to finish, they realized my hopes for the book and more.

I would also like to thank all the photographers who took the shots in this book, and in particular, John Dinkel, Dave Nicholas and the Binghamton Automobile Racing Club, Peter Luongo, Pete Lyons, Chris Perkins, D. Randy Riggs, Martin Rudow, Bill Warner, Evan Zema, and my wife, Ellen, who answered my requests for help in putting it together. A number of these shots are also gifts we received over the years.

I need more help than I would have on a project like this 20 years ago, and for that I would also like to thank my family, Shari Marks, and Cassandra Snyder.

Finally, the book has brought home to me how lucky I was in my career — most of all, maybe, for all the people of exceptional intelligence, warmth, and humor I had the chance to know.